T0064513

SACRED TEACHERS IN FUR

MYSTIC MEMOIRS

Adrienne Gallant

BALBOA.
PRESS

A DIVISION OF HAY HOUSE

Balboa Press books may be ordered through booksellers or by contacting:

Balboa Press
A Division of Hay House
1663 Liberty Drive
Bloomington, IN 47403
www.balboapress.com
1 (877) 407-4847

Because of the dynamic nature of the Internet, any web addresses or
links contained in this book may have changed since publication and
may no longer be valid. The views expressed in this work are solely those
of the author and do not necessarily reflect the views of the publisher,
and the publisher hereby disclaims any responsibility for them.

The author of this book does not dispense medical advice or prescribe the use
of any technique as a form of treatment for physical, emotional, or medical
problems without the advice of a physician, either directly or indirectly. The
intent of the author is only to offer information of a general nature to help
you in your quest for emotional and spiritual well-being. In the event you use
any of the information in this book for yourself, which is your constitutional
right, the author and the publisher assume no responsibility for your actions.

Any people depicted in stock imagery provided by Thinkstock are
models, and such images are being used for illustrative purposes only.
Certain stock imagery © Thinkstock.

Print information available on the last page.

ISBN: 978-1-5043-3828-8 (sc)
ISBN: 978-1-5043-3829-5 (e)

Balboa Press rev. date: 8/11/2015

To the Taffys of the world

and to Jessica, Dameon, and Rhiannon,

who still call me Maggie.

I have my quiet faith

and my ultimate trust

in God and my dogs,

and that's enough.

CONTENTS

Part III

PROLOGUE

Everyone's life is a story, a journey that starts at birth and, if all goes well, ends many years later. I believe we arrive with a blueprint—a plan for how we will survive and how we will choose our life's work—along with a list of lessons we wish to learn in earth school.

A theme runs like a river through each life, and as we fully awaken, we recognize our theme is being played out in sundry ways—or so it seems to me as I observe those who are living on purpose. If we have come here to learn and to master many lessons that fulfill our purpose—our theme— that implies there must also be many teachers.

This is my story. It is about my journey. It is about the wisdom of a goddess grandmother who, over the span of ten years, gifted a young goddess-in-the-making—me. This is also the story of seven sacred teachers who came to awaken me with all that has ever mattered: love and compassion.

These teachers came into my life over a span of thirty-five years and taught me invaluable lessons in terms of seeking truth. I sought answers to the mysteries of life and learned them from my sacred teachers in fur. The river of my life has led me to the ocean of love.

Be prepared to laugh and to cry as I recount how I learned to stand complete in my power as a woman while defining my ethical and spiritual values working with animals. I have developed self-love and self-appreciation through my work and have enjoyed every minute of it.

Since I was twelve, I have known that I am a goddess and have embodied the seven goddess archetypes in my personal awareness and awakening. Through the seven sacred teachers in fur, I have learned to have faith, courage, trust, and self-respect and have gained a final healing to reach my own special place of completeness.

Be warned: this story may open your heart much more than you dreamed possible! Tissues suggested.

But let's begin where I began. Here
is my story—and my truth.

PART I

Early Life

CHAPTER 1

A Hot July Morning—Maggie's Story

A baby girl was born in midsummer. After her fourth night on earth, she was carried at dawn—in a drawer filled with a soft, light-blue blanket—to a church in a remote New England town and placed on the vestry steps.

As the sun rose over the majestic White Mountains, a nun, one of three who lived in an upstairs dormitory at the church, finished her morning lauds, looked out of the window—open to the fresh, dewy air—and said, "Look, sisters. The sunrise is the color of tangerines today!"

At that moment, the three elderly nuns heard a baby crying down below. They rushed down many steps to find an old dresser drawer with an infant wrapped inside. The tiny baby weighed perhaps five pounds and was wearing nothing but a blue shirt that might have been more appropriate for a boy of two. It was buttoned left to right and had clearly

3

been previously worn. The dirty little shirt's pocket was embroidered with a puppy playing in some flowers, and in the pocket was a note that read, "Sisters, please watch over her. She was born four nights ago. We are gypsies, Irish and Welsh, and cannot raise her properly from the road. God bless you!"

And on that day the tangerine sun sent kisses to the earth!

The nuns were beside themselves, since their order had never required them to take in orphans, but clearly the tiny being in their midst needed to be fed immediately—needed clothes, diapers, shelter, and something other than a drawer to sleep in. The baby cried more loudly, presumably for her mother. The priest was summoned, and upon seeing the baby, he called the authorities, who were notorious for running gypsies out of town each summer (even though the gypsies always returned on trains to camp beneath the mountains and to do odd jobs at the local lodges and hotels). The authorities called the town doctor. All agreed that the baby would become a ward of the church and that they would wait a full year to see whether the child's family came back for her.

Word got out, and the parish found nursing mothers to assist. Baby clothes arrived by the carload, and the infant was placed in a donated crib. The nuns were delighted to have a little one to care for. They named her Mary Margaret Welsh, and the priest, Father Ted, lovingly nicknamed her Maggie. She was a healthy baby and spent most of the next year in her crib in the monastery.

An orphan is a child who has been abandoned by both parents or a young animal that has lost its mother.

The three nuns assigned themselves rotating eight-hour shifts to care for the baby. Doctor Putnam checked in every week. Maggie was nursed by different women from town who also did all her baby laundry. For the first three months, she cried frequently, as if she somehow knew that the women who came and went were not her own. She obviously missed her natural mother, and throughout her life, she always would. Nothing could change this fact. That is simply the way it is for orphans. Maggie was never carried far beyond the nursing chair, and she awoke many times in the dark and all alone. She cooed at the sound of church bells and of footsteps outside her little vestry alcove. Her first birthday came and went, but her original family never returned.

After one year and twenty-six days, a new woman came to the side of Maggie's crib and peered in. This woman was a social worker, and her arrival meant that the baby's birth family had not had a change of heart. So, at thirteen months, Maggie was put up for adoption. She had just started to sit up, but when she was put on her belly, she could only rock back and forth. Maggie did not have the strength to pull herself up to the side of her crib, so instead she sat there with her big brown eyes and tufts of wavy auburn hair, in hand-me-down clothes, and saw a second woman enter the room. Walking in behind her was a man who wasn't the priest or the doctor. This new woman picked her up, held her tightly, and kissed her sweet-smelling baby hair.

The woman said, "This is our baby."

The doctor said Maggie was fine to go home with them. The man could not hold the baby just yet, as he had been mountain climbing the previous week and had a case of poison ivy. The baby girl was fascinated with him, however, and gave him her first big smile, revealing two new teeth. Maggie left with the couple, squinting in the bright sunlight amid sprinkles of holy water, multiple blessings, and tears of farewell from Sisters Carol, Florence, and Marian and Father Ted, who all said they would never be the same. Indeed.

The couple, who had waited a long time for a baby of their own, were much older than most parents of a one-year-old. The baby gave a big yawn, cuddled into the woman's arms, and slept all one hundred miles back to her new home in Boston. The three were escorted out of town by the authorities, who said that in this case, no car seat was required.

That afternoon, Maggie tasted baby cereal and fruit for the first time and heard an Irish lullaby.

Each morning thereafter, she was placed on a big white sheet on the grass, and within two weeks, she had learned to crawl in the late-summer sunshine. Each night, someone rocked her to sleep on the porch under the moon and a sequined sky of stars, with fireflies lighting up the yard. The baby could see sunny days, moonlit nights, stars, grass, flowers, trees, birds, and bugs, but best of all, a mother and a father who had chosen her to complete their family. They showered her with love, toys, books, and beautiful music. They read to Maggie every night for the next eight years, even after she herself could read. Uncles, aunts, and cousins visited and adored this baby and even gave her a belated first-birthday party. It was quite a celebration. Maggie was now fourteen months old and was beginning to take her first steps.

Equally special to the little girl was the family dog, Sally, a black cocker spaniel. Sally slept in Maggie's room for the next five years and became her constant companion. Maggie was renamed Claire, after her mother's best friend, and baptized in the neighborhood Episcopal church, with godparents attending as well. Under the terms of her adoption, both parents were required to accompany her to a church of their choice whenever possible. For many years, the family walked across the street to Saint Andrew's Episcopal Church. Even though Claire's adoptive father was raised Catholic, he was a devout atheist. However, honoring the adoption agreement, he attended church. The god of all atheists must have smiled! Claire's parents loved her deeply, and she always felt safe with them. She could not have asked for a better childhood.

Her mother, who suffered from chronic insomnia, would stay up sewing many nights, and in the morning, Claire would have a new dress hanging on her doorknob. Her father taught her many words. A printer by trade, he would often leave a line of backward lead-type letters on the breakfast table for Claire to decipher. So much fun! These are just two of many examples of the love these great parents had for their adopted daughter.

The girl's namesake, her mother's best friend Claire, died from breast cancer at age forty-two. When the younger Claire turned forty, she renamed herself Adrienne, because she felt the sad energy of her namesake hovering over her.

She thought a name change would clear any pattern of an early death.

Maggie to Claire, Claire to Adrienne—same soul. Sometimes it's all in a name, and sometimes it isn't.

Claire always knew that she was adopted, but her parents did not tell her the story of her adoption until she turned twenty-five. They had asked her whether she was interested in finding her biological parents, and she said, "No. I have the best parents I could ever have in this world."

Claire now had the little blue shirt she wore at four days old. Wrapped in old tissue paper, it was a present for her twenty-fifth birthday.

CHAPTER 2

The River of Life—My Story

So this is how the river of my life started. I had a wondrous childhood: summers at the lake and winters skiing, sledding, and skating with an off-off-off-Broadway-actress mother and an Appalachian Mountains–climbing father. Our home was always filled with music and theater people who visited regularly from New York and with climbing enthusiasts from my father's circle of friends. But the best part of my childhood was when my maternal grandmother visited for three months every summer.

I spent my days with her while my mother went off to do summer stock. My father left after work on Fridays to be with my mother. He built all the sets for her plays, and Gram took me to see some of these productions. Gram also taught me to paint, and I took ballet lessons at Meadow Hearth, an outdoor stage in a meadow of wildflowers. I also had violin lessons, and each summer Gram and I planted strawberries that I sold at local farm stands. Gram always stressed that Mother Earth could feel us loving her this way.

During my eighth summer, Gram declared me an entrepreneur, a big word for someone my age, but by my eleventh summer, I was earning a lot of money and I felt proud and joyful doing my work. From that early point, I knew the value of being my own boss, and that gave me tons of confidence. This was a great gift from my grandmother. She told me that no matter what, I should always have my own money and that a woman with money can make powerful choices in life.

Gram was a girlie-girl. She always wore rubies and opals. One time we went purse shopping, and she told me never to buy a purse that cost more than what I had to carry in it! From that, I received a wonderful teaching: I didn't need to pretend I was anything I was not. An expensive purse might make me look richer, but my true worth had nothing to do with money. Of course, carrying an expensive leather purse contradicts all the values I have since developed. It amazes me that people never realize their big leather couches were once cows that were violently slaughtered to provide seats for humans. Ugh! Much later in my life, I adopted two cows from Sacred Cows Sanctuary in Gainesville, Georgia. Susan, the owner, told me of farms where the four- to six-month-old calves, weighing three hundred to four hundred pounds, would be taken for slaughter. The mother cows would moo in distress for days and nights afterward.

Gram had sage advice on almost every topic. On the subject of boys and men, she was fond of saying, "You can't live with them, and you can't live without them." She told me to be my own mate and to love myself first. A husband is just icing on the cake, but you don't need one, Gram said, adding that wants and needs are not the same. She said if I wanted to marry, "Pick a man who you would want any future children to have as their father, even if you don't want children. It's amazing how this narrows the field!" She also said, "Never ever run after a man. If he is worthy of you, he will find you."

Gram left for Florida each year in the fall, and oh how I missed her! I loved my parents, but my grandmother was special to me. She said, "Always say hello and smile at everyone you cross paths with. Don't leave one person out!"

She was a goddess not only in her physical beauty but in her wisdom. People would say that I looked just like my grandmother; this made me feel that I belonged to someone, an important consideration for an adopted child. Gram and I were somehow the same. This was long before all the talk about the law of attraction, but looking back, we were closely aligned with one another. I once asked her if she thought we were caught up in a big dream and really were not "here" at all. Calling me by her nickname for me, she said, "Yes, sweet face, this is all a dream, but it's God's dream, and all we have to do is our best while we're living here. Always be kind and life will unfold in the most joyful and wondrous ways. Always be true to yourself, and you will go far."

For my birthday in my eleventh summer, Gram gave me Taffy—not the candy but a little hound dog the color of a caramel sunset. She said that animals picked certain people to be with and that Taffy would comfort me when I was missing her after she left for Florida. She was right! Taffy and I were inseparable.

Gram and I exchanged weekly letters and wrote our thoughts in identical journals that we shared with one another each summer. Because of Gram, I love to write.

Here is how I answered security questions for my bank account.

Who is your childhood hero?

Grandmother

What is your favorite animal?

Dog

What is your favorite hobby?

Writing

I learned to read at four and started writing at five. When I was six, I would recite Edward Lear's poem "The Owl and the Pussycat" at women's club meetings. I have always adored public speaking.

Sarah Pope, our next-door neighbor, was eighty-three and came from North Carolina only in the summers. I visited her often and loved her house. She had hundreds of books that I liked to hold in my hands; I was fascinated by the gold-leaf edges on many of them. She asked me if I wanted to read them, and I thought I could, so she taught me how. I read aloud in the nicest Carolina accent; you can imagine my parents' smiles when they heard their New England child sounding like a proper southern belle.

It's easy to see how, even at age six, reciting the "The Owl and the Pussycat" over and over at small-town events, I was aligning myself with the magic of animals. Also note that the Pussycat asked the Owl to marry her! They were different species, but love is love. She knew what she wanted, and that was never lost on me.

Later, I wrote for my school paper, and over the years I've written many letters to the editor, short stories, children's books, and poetry. I also write articles for my website, www.roombyroomdecluttering.com.

On Thanksgiving of my twelfth year, my mother's only sibling—her brother—and his family came to visit from Delaware. It was almost like Gram was there, since this was her entire family now. My grandfather, her husband, had died when I was a baby. We had a wonderful New England holiday, but Saturday morning—two days after Thanksgiving—we got a phone call that would change my life forever. My grandmother had suffered a heart attack and died that morning. Two hours later, Taffy was out doing her rounds, and we heard a gunshot too close to our house. Everyone was crying about my grandmother when Taffy appeared at the door, leaving a trail of blood behind her in the snow. She had chased away a deer that a hunter was trying to kill. When my father found him in the woods, the hunter admitted that he got angry and shot Taffy instead. She died in my uncle's lap on the way to the vet.

I knew beyond a doubt that Taffy was trying to save the deer by chasing her away from the hunter. Taffy's very nature was love, unlike the hunter, who was toxic in his anger and frustration. This was my first "sacred teachers in fur" lesson. Animals are pure sources of love. They have no agenda; they are here to open our hearts. Maybe someday that hunter will awaken and understand that killing a child's pet will never get him a deer. But who knows?

In maybe a tenth of a second, I had had a glimpse of my alignment and my higher purpose, but it was not quite the right time to pursue this. Within five hours, I had lost my favorite person on the planet and my sweet, loving dog, and I was devastated and inconsolable for a long time.

All I remember about my grandmother's funeral a week later was laughing hysterically while one of my aunts held me to quiet me. When you are twelve years of age, grief is a strange emotion; it is at any age, really. I didn't return to school until January. My parents and my school gave me space to grieve. My mother took me to the movies almost every day. I will never know how she knew to do this, but it helped.

The following spring, instead of getting excited about a summer visit from Gram that would never happen again, I started seeing things. Some images were beautiful and some were frightening. The worst by far would start with the sound of footsteps heading up the stairs. When they stopped, I would look up from my pillow, and two clowns would be standing beside my bed with buckets of white paint to paint my face. To this day, clowns, even mimes, disgust me and I'm uncomfortable with Halloween masks.

Another image was of a woman floating down the hall by my bedroom. She was dressed in a blue gown and held a candle. I sensed her coming and woke up to the glow of the candlelight. She stopped in front of my door, smiled and nodded to me, and then disappeared. I saw bumblebees as big as Volkswagen Bugs and often saw what I have always called my golden dawn.

Outside of my bedroom was a porch, the special place where I could watch the rising sun in the morning and the moon and the stars at night. One morning when I went out to my porch, I saw golden light and golden beads of dew falling on our rose garden. Each rose petal lifted up a bit, as if to greet the dew. From that day on, I saw golden light everywhere, each sunbeam dripping in gold.

Then the best visions came. I woke up one night and Taffy was curled up asleep on my bed. She awakened and I said, "Oh Taffy, you're here!," but in a nanosecond, she was gone. The next night I stayed awake, hoping she would return, but instead, I saw my grandmother at my door. She blew me a kiss, and then she was gone.

Now I knew that Gram and Taffy were alive somewhere and had not died forever. Nothing would ever be the same. I had "knowing" and I believed with my whole heart that God had sent them back to me for a reason. My grief gave way to a feeling that I was no longer powerless. I started to travel in the astral realms, to Avalon-like places full of beautiful rivers, canyons, and lakes and once to a church in Spain. I knew there was so much more to this life. My secret hope was that I would fly to God, and I had so many questions for him/her/spirit/the universe/the light/Jesus/Buddha/ Muhammad/whoever! I came in knowing there was God, a source of everything, and have never had any doubts. In my thirteenth summer, I started reading everything I could find about the mysteries of life—*Autobiography of a Yogi*, Edgar

Cayce's writings, *The Bhagavad Gita*, *The Tao Te Ching*, the poetry of Rumi, to name a few.

My mother's birthday was soon to come. Gram and I had always shopped for her present together, but the summer before her passing, Gram had shopped alone. She left the gift wrapped on the top shelf of my closet, and it would be my job to give it to my mother. This was an emotional birthday for my mother. In her dramatic and always sweet way, with a smile on her face, said it was her first birthday as an orphan. After cake and ice cream, then flowers and candy from my father, I handed her Gram's present. Mother opened it and found a perfume called Heaven Scent. We all cried. I cried tears of joy because that was all I needed to prove we don't really die. I felt my grandmother right there and became ecstatically happy.

Soon I had my first boyfriend. I became a cheerleader, ran on the track team, and played field hockey. I was also voted treasurer of my class. It seemed that I was turning into a regular teenager, with one exception: I had a glorious secret! I knew that life was meant to be joyful. If I had managed to get here—*incarnate* was a new word in my young vocabulary—and to be adopted into a wonderful, loving, and supportive family, I reasoned that my life must have some purpose, and I knew it was not to suffer.

Every experience, no matter how bad it seems, holds within it a blessing of some kind. The goal is to find it.

—Buddha

Except for the day I had lost my dog and my grandmother, life had been lovely. Even in my pre-adoption days, I had been kept clean and safe and had been loved—maybe not in the standard ways that babies experience but loved by three nuns, a priest, and a small-town doctor. They were essentially my first family. Now we know that families can come in many forms, so to this day, I feel fortunate for those early experiences.

Another interesting revelation was gifted to me at age fifteen. As a result of Taffy being shot and killed by that hunter, I realized that animals are sacred and don't deserve to be killed for sport, for food, or as an outlet for anger. My mantra became "All life is sacred." How anyone could think that God would value one life over another is beyond me. Every part of creation has significance. If we do not value others, we do not value ourselves. Each soul is a part of the whole. Each of us is a petal on the same rose.

The rose is my favorite flower. Throughout my life, the scent of a rose has wafted in and out of my senses. Sometimes even on snowy days I smell roses. Long ago I saw how each petal in our family rose garden lifted itself to greet the dew, and this has made them special to me. Roses are a symbol of so many things. And I love symbols! The rose, a symbol of love and beauty, was called the queen of flowers by the Greek poetess Sappho.

So here we are in the Age of Aquarius, living in the third dimension on earth. The mission of animals is to open our hearts. They are love and compassion incarnate, and most people, when asked, admit that animals are better than humans. I will even go so far as to say our animals choose us. Many of us have an inexplicable recognition when we first see them, such as "That's my cat!" Animals come into total alignment with their purpose and can clear the path for a person in so many ways. You have seen your animal circle before it lies down. It is lining up with the earth's magnetic field and clearing psychic debris and stuck energy.

If my grandmother had not given me Taffy, and if Taffy had not been shot, I don't think I would have taken the path of animal rescue. I would not have met the other furry teachers who came to give me their sacred wisdom. Over the next thirty-five years, my life's theme would play out. My personal river—from orphan to goddess—would lead to the ocean of love. I knew that my destiny when I grew up would be to help all the Taffys I could. I also knew on the deepest level what it felt like to be defenseless, without a voice. Little did I know that even though I had been adopted—chosen, as it were—I still needed a lot more rescuing to reach my final goal: being in perfect alignment with my soul. I would rescue and would ultimately be rescued in return.

Life continued. I left for college, and although I missed my grandmother and my dog, I overcame my feelings of loss because I realized I had experienced unconditional love coming from Gram and Taffy even after their physical deaths.

As a tribute to my sweet dog, I often give a gift of taffy candy to my friends on birthdays or holidays. Now they'll know why!

I became a seeker, a searcher for truth. At age twenty-one, I went to India. When I returned, I joined and was initiated into a Sufi order, practicing for twelve years. I studied theology and became a minister. Over the next twenty years, I read every self-help book I could find. I knew in my heart that all life is sacred, that one soul is no more sacred than another, and that we are all one. There is no "them." It's all us! All paths, all lifetimes, lead back to the source—river to ocean. It can take a great many lifetimes with a great many experiences, but we will all eventually recognize who we are. We will also know that the best way to serve others is to maintain a sense of gratitude throughout our journey back home. In my world, all orphans eventually go home. As Oprah Winfrey says, "This is what I know for sure!"

I eventually married and had children of my own. Then I moved to Hawaii, where another gift presented itself. I awoke one morning, and my first thought was that I had intuitive *feng shui* knowledge as well as an innate understanding of an ancient practice called space clearing. That explained why I always felt a need to rearrange my family's furniture when I was growing up. I was actually clearing stuck energy at ten years of age! The gift of that morning's awakening became even more impressive when I also realized I had always been able to read energy, good and bad—good meaning flowing, bad meaning stuck. I thought everyone had that ability. Not so!

Feng shui simplified:

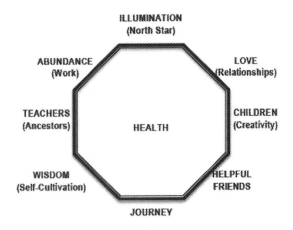

This is a *bagua* (ba-gwa) map, which guides objects within a space. It is a symbolic internal guidance system for maintaining a balanced life. Our homes reveal exactly where we are on our journeys of self-discovery. Each of the nine sections represents an essential element of life and holistic living. The quest for balance is a lifetime pursuit, and as we grow and change, so do our homes. We reflect our homes; our homes reflect us.

Immediately upon entering people's homes, I can read the energy by where they have placed furnishings and the stuff they have collected. I can observe the health section of a home and know if someone is ill or on a healing journey. I can look at the relationships section and know if a person is in love or missing someone. This is true for each *gua*, or section of a home.

My twelve-year marriage ended in divorce, and I became the sole (soul) supporter of my two daughters and myself. For the next eleven years, I had a career in public relations that came with great health insurance, a company car that I could also use on weekends, and a salary almost big enough to raise my family. As money got tighter, Gram's words echoed often: "Do what you love!" So I opened my own business on the side. I called it Room by Room. I decluttered and reorganized people's homes and helped to clear their endless mind chatter by offering tele-classes on forgiveness, awakening inner peace, becoming more authentic, and many other self-affirming subjects.

While I was doing this work at night and on weekends, I could hear something bigger calling me. I could feel an energy pulsating through me, a power both old and new. I was starting to understand some ancient truths. My grandmother had often said that when we know our truths, we must apply them and then we will be goddesses. I assumed I was feeling goddess energy, and I wanted this above everything else. But something seemed to be missing. I had traveled all over Asia as a seeker, and I had never doubted that God exists. Call that what you like: spirit, the universe, source energy, white eagle, mother and father God (my favorite), Adonai, Jehovah, and so on. Even so, there was a part of me that I could not reach.

Over the next twenty-five years I would learn that this missing part was buried deep within me. My true nature was in there somewhere, and it would require several teachers to guide me to what Hindus call *sunyata satchidananda*—the divine feminine. What I wanted to find was my divine feminine nature, best known as my authentic self. I figured if I had gotten myself into this lifetime, I had a purpose in being here, and I was determined to find it. There was so much more to discover, and I knew a path of suffering was never my soul's intention. But what was the opposite of suffering? So many people suffered; what was the purpose in all this suffering? Over the years my teachers showed up, and they came in fur. From them, I learned why we are here and found out that the opposite of suffering is something quite magnificent!

So here are the stories of seven dogs that represented seven goddess archetypes and helped me to become my true self and to discover my life's purpose.

The seven archetypes are:

• Warrior queen

- Sacred sage

- Natural healer

- High priestess

- Primordial mother

- Daring diva

- Magical muse.

I have become each of them.

PART II

The Dogs' Stories

CHAPTER 3

Holly's Story of Courage

It was Christmastime, and my two daughters and I had returned to California from Hawaii, all in deep grief. The man of my dreams, whom I had met in college twelve years before, had betrayed me dozens of times; to stay would have been to betray myself. So I had no choice but to start over and to build a different kind of life. The grief came from the fact that the girls, ages seven and eleven, would never have a relationship with their father. I divorced him, and he divorced them. He never again made an effort to include them in his life.

Enter Holly—a midsized, black cockapoo, Benji-like, scruffy, cuter than cute, and also in deep grief. She had been left on a roadside in a crate with two puppies, all rescued by the local ASPCA. The puppies were adopted three weeks later, and Holly was alone in a big kennel on death row, even though she had committed no crime. This was a kill shelter, and the people running the place kept dogs for six weeks, period. Holly had only a few days left. They estimated her age to be around ten months, She was a puppy herself! As Holly shivered in the back of the all-cement kennel, I went to the front desk and paid her ticket to love and freedom. We left smiling because we had found the perfect dog for my parents. They were celebrating their retirement and a recent move to Pacific Grove, California. After having Holly groomed, and decorated with a big red bow, we drove off the next day.

We were excited to be having a traditional Christmas; it was hard to feel Christmasy in Hawaii. When we arrived, it was love at first sight for Holly and my father, and the girls and the new dog settled in for a holiday lovefest. My father was in Santa mode, and Hawaii was almost forgotten.

After five days of too many presents and too much food, it was time to say good-bye, and oh how the tears flowed! I finished packing the car while the girls walked Holly one more time. We got into the car, and my mom and dad positioned themselves on the driveway to wave good-bye. As we were pulling out, my dad said, "Wait a minute. I need to get my camera." Instead, he came out with Holly. He had put her red bow back on and said to me, "I think you forgot someone. She is clearly your dog; I'm her grandfather, but I will be too busy working at the lighthouse." Dad had given up mountain climbing for a new career as a lighthouse aficionado, and after visiting about one hundred lighthouses, he started writing about their history. His biggest interest was writing about women lighthouse keepers. My mother referred to them as "the other women."

I said, "Are you sure?" He didn't answer but put Holly and her bed in the back of the car with the rest of the presents. For the next thirteen years, Holly had new puppies to care for: we became hers and she watched a seven-year-old and an eleven-year-old become twenty and twenty-four and witnessed everything that growing up in an all-girl family entailed. I should say a family of girlie-girls directed by a femme-fatale single mother ready for the challenge of raising girls who would grow up strong and independent and who would rely on much more than their looks, which were and still are exquisite.

At times I'm sure we qualified for food stamps, but I never accepted that. As long as I could work, we would have enough to eat. We never had extras like cookies and chips, but we did enjoy ice cream cones every Friday. Everyone would be waiting on our doorstep for me to get home from work—Holly included! She had a scoop of vanilla every Friday. All we had to say was "ice cream" and she headed for the car. My daughters understood the importance of a strong work ethic and knew that studying hard promised all kinds of good results later in life. But just as my grandmother had taught me, I taught them to slow down and to work only at the things they loved. I encouraged them to take time to identify those passions, and they did just that.

We discovered that Holly liked being read to, and she would often sprawl across a bed and listen to homework being recited. A neighbor heard about this and gave Holly her own subscription to the *Wall Street Journal*—very funny! Somehow Holly knew the paper was hers, and she would carry it in from the postbox and set it down in her toy bin. We renamed her newspaper the *Holly Wolly Polly Froggy Doggy Journal*, and her little tail would almost wag off when we would say it.

Another fond memory was when she came home from the vet after being spayed. One of her favorite spots to sleep was my closet. It was warm and carpeted, and following her surgery, that's where she wanted to be. After a couple of hours, I went into my room to check on her and became concerned. I said, "Oh Holly, you're shaking!" She lifted a paw. Someone had loved her enough to teach her how to shake paws. Maybe whoever had let her go didn't want to do it but had no choice. Maybe this person's life was such that caring for her or her puppies would have been impossible. Maybe the person was too young to know yet or too old to know how anymore. At that moment on a Friday night, three thousand miles away from my birthplace, I felt with all my heart what a plight my own first family must have faced in deciding that someone else would have to care for me. These people, like Holly's first family, hoped I would get a better life.

> **We have come into this exquisite**
> **world to experience ever more deeply**
> **our divine courage and light.**
> **—Hafiz**

This was a huge act of courage in what must have felt like terrible circumstances. And Holly and I did, as it turned out, get much better lives. As I sat with her on the floor of my closet, I cried and Holly, always the mother, lapped away my tears. She wasn't shaking anymore; there was too much kissing for that!

Once again, I was reminded of the power of love. Somehow this young, single parent and this little dog would be able to handle whatever came their way. And what came next for this little dog was her first summer vacation. I took my two weeks of vacation every July and rented a cabin at Lake Tahoe. Each daughter could bring a friend, and often my mother would join us. So there were usually six of us and Holly. It turned out that Holly loved to swim. She had her own beach towel and would lie in the sun after a swim like the rest of us. By the end of our vacation, everyone else on the beach knew Holly's name, since she liked to visit all beach blankets and everybody lying on them. She also got more treats and beach toys than you would find in Petco!

Holly made all our vacations so much fun. One year, my father wasn't feeling well, so my mother could not join us. At about midnight, Holly was barking hysterically at the window. I looked out and saw that two cars had arrived, carrying several teenagers. My older daughter, who was turning fifteen, swore she had invited only two people. (We got through that little fib.) I asked all of them to call their parents to tell them where they were. They ordered pizza and slept in the huge living room after swimming at midnight and staying up all night, talking, laughing, and playing board games. When I got up the next morning, Holly was not in her bed. My younger daughter and her friend were not in their room. Everyone, including Holly, was asleep in front of the fireplace! Holly looked up and saw me, and that tail thumped loudly as if to say, "Hi. I went to a party!" I said, "Yes, you did!"

We got through those teenage years and also my dating years, as I call them now. Holly was with me through it all. I was asked out a lot, but my girls came first. I remembered my grandmother quoting Confucius: "Wherever you go, go with all your heart." My girls had all my heart every day. Only three men in ten years caught my fancy. One was a screenplay writer, and that relationship lasted two years. The second was an actor and a singer. Maybe I was channeling my mother: actors, singers, writers—oh my! Anyway, he loved Holly and thought she should audition for the part of Toto in Beach Blanket Babylon's version of *The Wizard of Oz* in San Francisco.

We arrived for the auditions at 4 p.m. and were given a number, and at 10 p.m., we were finally called to the stage. Holly looked the part, but we were both exhausted, and when they asked her to sit, she barked; when they asked her to come, she froze, and when they asked her to speak, she sat down. We were disqualified on the spot amid lots of laughter from the crowd watching. However, Holly appeared happy with herself, and when we returned to the car, I looked deep into her eyes and got a clear message: of course she knew all the commands, but she was her own dog—no one could make her do anything. We could never have kept the rehearsal schedule even if she had passed the audition. Holly saved us both a lot of time and energy, and we avoided falling into the abyss of the acting world.

After her audition, Holly slept for two days. It took a lot out of her to make me understand that I was trying to fit into a world I had no energy for. And this actor I thought I was in love with proved to be as empty as that stupid audition. (By the way, a weimaraner won the audition. Do you think a weimaraner looks like Toto? Neither do I.) Holly never did anything she didn't want to do, and from that point forward, I spent a lot more time becoming clear about what I wanted to do. Beach Blanket Babylon's version of the Yellow Brick Road was not my path, although I would eventually meet the Wizard and reclaim all my power. By now it was evident that Holly had found me as much as I had found her. I don't think my ten years of being a single parent would have been the same without my third girl.

My dad seemed to understand that I needed Holly more than he did. Still, on many occasions he would drive from Pacific Grove to do research at the Maritime Museum in San Francisco, arriving to pick up the girls for a long weekend before I got home from work. He always left a sweet note: "The four of us are on our way back to your mother; will call when we get there." This meant Holly was going to spend three full days with him. She loved the beach but never went in the ocean.

Our house came with a pool, which helped to keep the girls at home, since ours was the house all the kids loved to visit. One morning around six, I let Holly out in the backyard while I was making coffee and lunches and getting us ready for school and work. By eight, the girls had left, and I was preparing Holly's breakfast. At this point she was usually under my feet, but that morning she didn't enter the kitchen.

I went outside to find her and heard a pitiful whimpering. The gate to the pool had been left open, and Holly was treading water—with a baby skunk barely afloat nearby! She must have chased it into the pool. I had to lift her out, because the steps were more of a ladder and not built for animals. I wrapped her in a towel and put her on a chaise lounge while I got a net and scooped out the skunk, which appeared to be almost drowned. I called work to say I wouldn't be in and rushed Holly to the veterinarian. She was okay, just awfully tired. When we returned home, the baby skunk was nowhere to be seen. I stayed home all day and cuddled with Holly between naps, and even though it was Tuesday, she had ice cream. The following summer at Lake Tahoe, she didn't go in the water even once, and she never swam again. Lesson learned!

The years passed, and one spring day, Holly went out for her morning routine but never returned. She had died in the yard. The vet surmised that she had suffered a stroke. At fourteen, my girl was gone. Even though I knew that death is not forever, the shock of her going so quickly was beyond anything I had felt, including my divorce and the recent passing of my father. I sobbed for days and days. I missed her. My girls cried, the groomer cried, our neighbors cried. My boss said, "It's just a dog." And that day, I quit my job. Thank you, Holly!

I could, from that point forward, be free to work at what I loved. I didn't need a company car or a 401(k). From that day on, I would never have to seek permission to go to the bathroom, take a lunch meeting convenient for someone else's schedule, or arrange a vacation based on the office hierarchy or on seniority.

The girls were grown; I didn't need to insure them through an employer. I would join Kaiser, and I vowed I would never have another dog.

We buried Holly's ashes under her favorite tree at her favorite park, overlooking a rose garden. Her collar and tags are in my special box (remember the story of the littlest angel?), and her photo is on my writing desk. She left a few months after my dad, and through oceans of tears, I knew they would be together that Christmas.

Being deeply loved gives you strength;

loving deeply gives you courage.

—Lao Tzu

Thank you, Holly, my sacred teacher. I learned how to be courageous from your example.

My time with Holly brought out in me the goddess archetype of the primordial mother. I am all about love and compassion. I own self-love, self-respect, and self-appreciation. My heart is open. I think love. I am love.

CHAPTER 4

Tulip's Story of Authenticity

Three years had gone by since Holly's passing, and I could feel that another dog was trying to come into my life. I sensed a calling, so I went to the local shelter—just to look.

Tulip was a five-month-old border collie. She was larger than normal, and I would learn she also had a large spirit to contain. Tulip and her three brothers had found themselves at the local Humane Society after the Fourth of July when loud fireworks had sent them running. Their owner never looked for them, so they were put up for adoption. The male puppies were adopted first, leaving Tulip on death row. She had a week left, and I had to jump through hoops to get her. At the time I did not have a fenced yard, so I had a friend with a yard adopt her and bring her to me. (In this lifetime, I would lie, steal, and beg to get any animal to safety.) This was a simple decision: Tulip called, and I answered. During the next eleven years, Tulip was all mine and I was hers. She was like a wild pony wearing feathered and spotted leggings; she had long fur and was stunning.

The minute I saw Tulip, I recognized a part of myself—my wild side, tamed for no good reason. If people could have an animal soul mate, she was mine. Like Holly, she grew up with my daughters, now of college age, visiting with their boyfriends. There was also a Mr. Right in my life again, and Tulip loved him as well.

Tulip had the best life a border collie without a herd of sheep could ask for. Together we were like two wild roses, going in every which way. We could read each other's hearts, and we shared otherworldly experiences. People would say, "You two are a match made in heaven." And they had no idea! Leashes were unnecessary—for either of us. Tulip was the free spirit I had longed to be prior to my single-parenting days. Looking back, perhaps a little training might have been helpful, though I'm not certain either of us could have been taught anything new. We were like free agents waiting for our next assignment. I spent lots of time exercising her. She needed to run and had enough energy for three dogs.

Then the light-bulb moment! Surely there were others whose dogs needed to get out of the house while their families were at work or school. Maybe Tulip and I could be together all day—working! For the next nine years, she and I ran a dog walking/hiking/pet-sitting service in Marin County, California, with more than three hundred dogs in my clientele. I put up one flyer, and the first day, I received five calls that turned into my first five clients. I never had to advertise again and did business entirely by word of mouth for nine years. I could serve people and dogs! This was a perfect line of work for me, and I could be outside, enjoying nature.

My flier read:

Adrienne's All-Weather K-9 Hiking Club.

Hike (n.): A long country walk

I love dogs and believe that the happiest dogs get out to see the world, and other dogs, every day. If you agree, then call me to set up a time that's best for you and your pet.

—Adrienne

In addition to dog walking and pet-sitting, I offered therapeutic massage, transportation to and from the vet or groomer, social activities and pet birthday parties, swimming, basic grooming, and much more. I quit my two part-time jobs: one selling art and another cooking in a vegetarian restaurant. I crossed those things off of my bucket list.

Tulip was a working dog, and we were well known all over the county. My calendar was full. Tulip took this work as seriously as I did, and in my K-9 hiking club, she led the group. The other dogs looked up to her, and she called the shots. If a dog wandered from the trail, all I had to say was, "Tulip, where's Sam (or whoever)?," and she would herd him back to the group—but only after she had had a romp off of the trail herself! While Holly had been a girlie-girl dog, Tulip was a wild child. She was beautiful and had a queen-bee energy. Over and over again, she gave me the gift of seeing how my own beauty and feminine energy could feel wild and how natural this was. She was a sweet soul with a large personality.

Everyone loved Tulip, and at holiday time, my clients abundantly gifted both of us. We were given three days in a chalet in Tahoe, and one Christmas we somehow got booked into a twelve-room "cabin" near Heavenly Valley Ski Resort! We could look out of our windows and see people skiing only ten feet away. Tulip loved watching the skiers. Of the twelve rooms, she chose the top one, up four flights of stairs, sleeping away from us in her own double bed. She looked like she had finally found the bedroom she had always dreamed of.

One of Tulip's quirkiest traits was that she often hardly seemed to be a witness to her own life. She was in her own bliss and clearly on her own path of freedom. During these spells, she never ate two times a day like most dogs. Sometimes she would go a day and a half or more between meals. At other times, she ate regularly, but only when she felt like it—almost as if to say, "Routines are for the unadventurous." Then, "Oh yeah, I'm hungry now. I 'forgot' to eat earlier." Many people said she should eat more regularly, but in Tulip's world there were no *shoulds*. She seemed to thrive and could live on fun and long walks for a long time. She taught me this, and I let go of my million *shoulds*.

At this stage of my life, I could do whatever I chose to do. My girls were grown, and the man in my life—my Mr. Right—placed few demands on my time. However, I was becoming keenly aware of our differences. For instance, we ate very differently: he was a big Texan and was used to having longhorns on the table; I was a vegetarian, so we cooked our own meals. He was loud; I was quiet, and while Tulip could adapt to both our personalities, I knew she favored me over him and would rather be with me, away from all his noise.

I was beginning to feel the same way, and I realized that if I wasn't experiencing love and passion, I was not being true to myself (recalling my grandmother's admonition).

I was falling in love with Tulip's energy and falling out of love with Mr. Right. Tulip's love was unconditional and at a higher frequency, whereas this man's love was clearly conditional, and I didn't gel with his frequency, his vibes. He made me uncomfortable. Tulip was always authentic, but I was not. I felt split. I needed to own my real feelings, and I could sense Tulip was trying to teach me this. What better way for me to do this than by finally admitting that once again, I was not being true to myself?

I have always been an extraordinarily tidy person. I don't function well with unnecessary stuff. My homes have always had an organic and Zen feel to them; they have been quietly beautiful. Mr. Right had layers and layers of stuff—all vital to him for his own reasons. I wanted to hire a Dumpster and throw it all away! He had even brought his childhood dresser all the way from Texas to California. A small, four-drawer affair made of plywood, it looked sweet. This was the same man who bought me a steamer trunk that came from England in the 1800s, ended up in Nebraska, and then in Half Moon Bay at an antique shop. I loved it! The trunk still felt full of hope. On my birthday, this expensive piece was in my living room, tied up in a big white bow—a total surprise. He did so many things like this. However, while Mr. Right was kind and generous, he was too big and noisy and was a clutter bug. Sadly, I couldn't admit to myself that I was not in love with him—and we were together for almost eighteen years! I still had a long way to go to be the best version of myself, a long way to go to be fully true to myself.

My first corporate job after returning from India was in public relations, and without it I could not have afforded to raise two daughters alone and to give them a decent life. My main expertise was in trouble-shooting. I was the one sent in to straighten out all kinds of disagreements. I did this during the years I had Holly, long before Tulip, but one of Tulip's amazing qualities was that she would try to break up fights and squabbles between dogs. She could quickly determine which dog was at fault, distract them, and keep an eye on whoever did not want to give up the fight. My sweet trouble shooter would put her body between them. The dogs saw her as the boss. I liked to believe she was an extension of me, but they looked to her for behavior modification. She looked to me, so it all worked out.

Tulip wanted to please me, and the other dogs seemed to want to please her. When we arrived at the dogs' homes, she and I both went to the door to gather our charges. Tulip waited until the other dogs were safely in the back before she got into the car. She rode shotgun, and pity the dog that thought it might like to ride in front with me! All she had to do was give a low growl, and it was three dogs in the back and Tulip in the front. I never took more than three clients at a time, since that was what I felt was safe and what Tulip and I could manage. I usually had fifteen dogs a day: five packs of three plus Tulip. Also, some dogs couldn't go out with other dogs. I did not allow Tulip into the homes where I did pet sitting. Her job was to watch the car, and she loved to stretch out in the back, off duty, and was often in deep sleep when I returned.

As Tulip got older, she wanted to be back at home by three, so our days started at six in the morning. By six in the evening, Tulip was asleep for the night. A lot of the job was brain work, and she got weekends off as well. I did pet-sitting most weekends, and I missed her, but even on weekends, her preferred bedtime was 6 p.m. As Mr. Right pointed out, many times I too loved to go to bed early, while he would stay up for hours. Tulip and I loved our sleep. We needed that restoration for our intense days.

I also operated a K-9 cookie business during the Tulip years, and though she was never a treat-oriented dog—she worked for love, not for food—she was my cookie tester. She and I had befriended a neighbor of one of my dog clients, who like everyone else, had fallen in love with Tulip. Gina was eighty-five at the time, and she bagged up all my cookie orders. I would get up at 4 a.m., bake several dozen batches, and drop them off at her house for packaging. I would pick them up the next day for delivery. Gina wouldn't take any money and said that her pay was in knowing Tulip and me. I gifted her with little things that she enjoyed, but money was never exchanged.

Like me, Gina had traveled all over Asia and had an intuitive knowledge of feng shui similar to mine. She had dedicated a table in her living room for the cookie packaging. The room was blessed by Kuan Yin statues and a beautiful fabric on the wall that matched the purple, rose, and orange of the ribbons that I used to attach my business cards to the bags. Each bag made a wonderful presentation, and Gina and I enjoyed many a dinner at her favorite Thai restaurant to celebrate every new account. All the money we made went to rescue organizations.

This was a beautiful time in my life and in Tulip's. I know that Gina loved to feel needed, and I could not have succeeded without her. Though we were forty years apart in age, we had a lot in common. We were Thelma and Louise in many ways. I fondly remember her saying, "What kind of trouble can we get into today?" We spent at least one afternoon together every two weeks or so, and I always came away feeling richer for knowing her. We settled all the world's problems with wonderful conversations on many topics. Four o'clock in the afternoon easily turned into seven, eight, or nine o'clock in the evening; more often than not, a pizza or burritos would mysteriously arrive around five-thirty. Gina would make tea and bring out her best china.

She would gift me a magazine subscription every year—*National Geographic* or *Better Homes and Gardens*, for example—and buy one for Tulip in her name, either *Dog Fancy* or *Bark*. Tulip, like Holly with her *Wall Street Journal*, got excited when our magazines arrived. For some reason, Tulip equated magazine reading with a massage, and when I would curl up to read, she would sit in front of me with her back to me and stay like that until I rubbed her shoulders for a while. Only afterward would she settle down and let me read.

For nine years, Tulip and I worked side by side until we moved out of Marin County up to Mount Shasta, located in quiet, scenic Siskiyou County. We both needed a big change. My heart was drawing me toward volunteer animal rescue work, and it was also time to leave the traffic and the movie-star lifestyles for a more peaceful place.

One of our last adventures before we left Marin was with a dog named Reuben. He was a Dalmatian, sweet but a bit hyper. That day, Tulip was tired, so I planned to walk Reuben by himself and to let Tulip sleep in the car. Reuben was not comfortable with other dogs, so I booked him as my last client on each of his five days during the week. This was perfect for me, since I could unwind a bit with just one dog—always on a leash—before going home, and Tulip was fine not walking with us. However, when we arrived at Reuben's house, his person was sobbing wildly, saying that Reuben had gotten out of the yard to chase a deer up into a vast forest behind the house. Instinctively, I knew what we had to do. I returned to the car and found Tulip wide awake. I let her out, pointed toward the woods, and said, "Tulip, go find Reuben!" And off she went. Ten minutes later, she was herding him home. I knew Reuben would smell Tulip's scent, hear her, and come out from wherever he was to see her, and I was right.

Tulip and I always spoke the language of the heart. She knew exactly what was needed. To this day I believe she had the most beautiful heart I may ever know. Her eye contact with everyone was precise: she never backed down or gave up. She was true blue in everything.

On another one of our last days of work, we went to the house of Tulip's best friend, Amber. Tulip had known Amber for a long while, since Amber was my third client. She was a reddish field retriever, a purebred girl who ate turkey every day of her life and smelled just awful! Tulip didn't care, and I was used to it. Amber and Tulip loved one another, and that was the most important thing. Amber loved to swim and had her own pool. (Marin County, remember?) Tulip would sit on the second step but never went into the water. In eleven years, she never swam, although she would lie in a kiddie pool on the deck at our house on hot days.

That day, she and Amber were running around the pool, chasing balls and Frisbees, when all of a sudden, splash! Tulip had fallen into the deep end of the pool and was flailing around like she was drowning. Amber got to her first and kept circling her, trying to show her how to dog paddle, a skill Tulip had never been remotely interested in learning. Finally, they got close to one side, and I reached in and pulled Tulip out. If this had gone on for a few more minutes, I would have been in that pool myself! Tulip shook off the water and immediately wanted to return to the car, so I put Amber back in her house. After that incident, whenever we visited Amber, Tulip stayed far away from the pool.

Tulip loved all the dogs in our clientele, but Amber was her favorite. Her second longtime friend and favorite dog pal was Benny Gooddog. Benny was a Norwegian elkhound and was also a solo walker, but we saw him only twice a week. Benny was gorgeous with his silver fur and black face. He was good off a leash, so he, Tulip, and I would hike all the way up his favorite trail on Mount Tamalpais. When we got in the car, Benny and Tulip romped and played in the back seat like six-week-old puppies. I'm sure people in passing cars wondered, *What the hell?*, as the two dog heads bobbed up and down while we rode to the trailhead. When we arrived, the dogs would be covered in one another's saliva. The dog world can be a messy one indeed! On the way home, they would be tired from all the running and romping, so Tulip would settle into the front passenger seat next to me, and Benny would stretch out to sleep in the back. Benny and Amber were the only other dogs allowed to be untethered in the car. Tulip insisted that they be free. I heard this from her, loud and clear. She didn't have to micromanage them like all the other dogs, so her time with them must have been wonderful for her.

Just before our move to Mount Shasta, I took Tulip to a dog park. We had wound down from our work, but I felt that she still needed to be with other dogs. I also knew that people I loved would be there, so it was a good opportunity to say more good-byes. I had one special friend, Larry, an eighty-year-old man with three dogs: an ancient retriever named Mo, a chocolate Labrador retriever named Troy, and a much younger dog, a rottweiler-Lab mix named Huey Lewis. That day, the real Huey Lewis was at the park with his little dog. (Talk about the power of love!) Larry had never met him and was not a music buff, but he had heard the name somewhere and had named his dog Huey Lewis. Marin County was full of dogs named Santana, Anne (Lamot), Joyce (Maynard), and George (Lucas). A lot of boxers were named Barbara, after the California senator, and on it went. I introduced Larry to Huey, and Huey to Huey, and it was great fun for all and so sweet for our good-bye day. Larry and I kept in touch until he died.

The next day, Tulip and I packed for hours and needed a break, so we visited another dog park for a short time. As we were leaving, an elderly woman and her daughter were entering through the gate with two Samoyeds. They are fluffy white dogs with bushy tails curled over their backs and always look like they are smiling. I had put Tulip on her leash, since we would be crossing a busy parking lot. Then bam! The Samoyeds saw her, cornered her, and attacked. They got caught up in her leash. The older woman reached in to pull her dogs away and was bitten. The younger woman screamed at me that my dog had bitten her mother. I said that I doubted it and that she should take better care of her dogs by keeping them on leash when entering the park. If you have ever heard dogs fighting, you know how high your adrenaline can go.

I got Tulip into the car and returned to see how bad the bite was. The younger woman said she would sue me, have my dog put down, and do a lot of other hideous things. They contended it had to be Tulip who bit the mother, since their dogs had no teeth! Okay, this was getting dicey, so I said, "Take your mother to the ER and call me, and I will pay for her visit." The mother said, "No, no. It's okay," but the daughter insisted and called me that evening to tell me the bill was $140. No stitches were required, but the ER doctor had to report a dog bite to the county animal officer, and sure enough, at eight the next morning, the quarantine unit was parked in my driveway. After knocking heavily on the door, an animal control officer demanded to see Tulip's rabies and vaccine records, which were all up to date, and she was placed in quarantine for two weeks. He said I could keep her on the back deck, but she was not to be around people or other dogs. What a way to end nine years of work! So twice a day, I had to put her on a leash and walk her out to the driveway to do her business.

On the fifth day, an officer came to check on us to be sure we were following orders. The daughter called to ask me how I liked quarantine, and I started crying over the phone. She yelled at me, "Stop crying like a little girl!" The situation was out of my control; the Taffy years came back into focus, and I finally cried the tears I had swallowed for thirty years. The day Tulip was to be freed from this stupid punishment, another animal control officer came by with paperwork for me to sign and said, "Tulip now has a record in Marin County; she will be put down if she bites another person." At that moment, Tulip went up to the officer, lay down at her feet, and nibbled at her boots! Luckily, the officer had a slight sense of humor and we laughed. The following week, Tulip and I made our final rounds to say good-bye to everyone. This took three days, and I gave everyone the names of dog walkers and pet-sitters whom I trusted. Many gifts, hugs, and kisses were exchanged; email addresses were updated, and off we went.

Mount Shasta, to me, is one of the most special places on earth. Tulip loved it too, and she especially enjoyed going to a place on the mountain called Bunny Flats, which is around 6,500 feet above sea level. But her favorite place was the uppermost plateau at nine thousand feet above sea level. We spent many a day up there alone with Tulip off leash. She seemed like a different dog there, almost like she wasn't in her body. Sometimes she would stand on top of one of the picnic tables, her fur blowing in the whistling wind, her eyes resting on me, and I would feel the closest to heaven I have ever felt.

Tulip, who was love incarnate, passed away six months later, at age eleven, on March 15, the day we had designated as her birthday. The vet who came to the house was named Grace, and it was her birthday too! Tulip's ashes are spread on her mountain, and her collar and eleven years of tags are in my treasure box. There were no border collies in my clientele, and for nine years, she was my queen bee. Within three days, after word got out to my clients in Marin of her passing, our home was filled with vast bouquets of tulips. So much love!

During this time, I was still seeing things, like a shadow walking across a room or big red balls of energy—which I have since learned are thought forms—that would roll through my house and burst with a loud pop. Even now, I occasionally experience a bit of discomfort when entering huge stores, since the energy is moving so fast that I often have to sit down. I've accepted that at some point I must have opened a portal to these phenomena. When I would see someone who wasn't there or hear a big, explosive sound, Tulip would stare in the direction of this form or this sound, but never react or engage.

On the way to Nelson, British Columbia—one of my favorite places on the planet—we stayed at a bed-and-breakfast in Spokane, Washington. A sweet little gray-and-white cat liked to sit in the hallway outside our door. This cat would walk around my legs when I opened the door. There was only one important issue in describing the cat's behavior: I was the only one who saw her! I have also had many a scream dream that would wake up everyone except my dogs, who always slept through them. This led me to believe that our pets live, and possibly sleep, in another realm. One exception occurred when Tulip was about three years old. I awoke one morning to the beautiful sound of a choir singing the word *joy*—just that one word. Tulip was there, and I know in my heart that she heard it too. This experience was something special that only she and I shared, and I think of it often as one of my life's miracles.

Tulip taught me to be my truest self. She introduced me to my journey into authenticity. She seemed to be in this world but not of it. I know she came into being just for my benefit, and I can't wait to see her again when my time comes. I know she will be waiting for me. Tulip brought out my high priestess. As a high priestess, I know my calling and I honor my destiny. I know there is a greater purpose beyond earthly concerns.

Thank you, Tulip, my sacred teacher.

CHAPTER 5

Lizzie's Story of Resilience

For about six years while I had my dog-walking/pet-sitting business, Lizzie was a client. She was a purebred Aussie, as pretty and poised as any dog could be and tricolor (black, white, and tan). This was appropriate, since I would learn there was nothing simply black and white about this girl's life. I am not sure how astrology plays into the lives of animals, but she was the only dog I ever knew who had a real-time birth date. The dates for all the others were approximate, as rescues, like orphans, have no beginning records regarding time of birth or health history.

Lizzie came from a breeder in Connecticut and was born on September 28—a Libra. And like many Libras, she was about balancing life's pros and cons. Her original mother-owner shared the same birthday, and they loved each other. The rest of her human family—a traveling husband

and two socially overbooked teenagers—could take her or leave her. All in all, these sweet people had not allowed their wealthy circumstances to exclude Lizzie, but because they traveled so much, they often referred to their home, a mansion with seven bathrooms, as Lizzie's doghouse. They were rarely home, so I became Lizzie's sitter, often for three to six weeks at a time. Lizzie was like a sister to Tulip and a second dog for me. So when we moved away from Marin, my only choice was to offer to adopt Lizzie, since there was no one else to care for her.

After we settled in Mount Shasta, I drove back to Marin and home again with some precious cargo: Lizzie and her "brother," a huge calico tomcat named Kitty, who also needed a new home. Kitty purred and drooled the entire way. I found another home for Kitty, and Lizzie adjusted beautifully to living with Tulip and me. I believe she never wanted to go back, although her original owners requested that we always think of Lizzie as having two families. They never visited but did keep up via emails for a year or so. I sent photos and they sent money for her care, which was very loving. For another five years, Lizzie would be mine, and little did we know of the adventures awaiting us.

Tulip was used to Lizzie going back home at some point during the pet sitting years, so she made it clear to Lizzie and me that while she knew it was important for Lizzie to be with us, she was still number one, the queen bee, the highest dog in all hierarchies. Lizzie never questioned or challenged this, especially since Tulip communicated her supremacy with occasional low growls. Lizzie understood Tulip's majestic nature, and since Lizzie was a "peace at any price" kind of dog, it all worked out. So Lizzie was with us for the last four months of Tulip's life, and I would see them together, sitting across the room from one another, clearly communicating.

Tulip knew before anyone else that her work with me was nearing completion, and looking back, I can see how she was passing the reins to Lizzie. After Tulip's departure, I had to keep going for Lizzie, though those first months were so sad for me. Whenever I cried, Lizzie would throw up. I later learned from an animal communicator that when

Lizzie's original human mother cried, it meant the family would be away traveling, and Lizzie always felt that these people were going to abandon her and never return. I think her human mother cried because she wasn't as keen about traveling as her husband was. When I cried, this confused Lizzie, and her reaction was to vomit out of fear of being left behind. After learning that about her, whenever I needed to cry about anything, I would sit in my car so Lizzie could not see or hear me, and she never vomited again.

Five to eight months later, Daisy and Charlie entered our lives. Daisy came in October, and Charlie followed in February of the following year. Lizzie and I were out walking when the sweetest white-and-tan puppy followed us home. I put her in the yard before going into the house to call the animal shelter to see if I could bring her there, but before I could make the call, Mr. Right, who had moved with us to Mount Shasta, came out of his garage office, looked at her, and said, "You found my dog." This came from a man who, when I first met him, said he was a cat person and didn't even like dogs! I said we had to search for her owner, and

I drove her to the shelter. But after five days, no one came looking for her, so we adopted her and named her Daisy. She had an affinity for Mr. Right and was clearly his dog. She had chicken-like bones sticking out everywhere, but no dog was ever sweeter than Daisy.

A few months later, Lizzie, Daisy, and I were on one of our walks and came across another stray dog—no collar, no tags—who followed us home. Lizzie had a look in her eyes, as if to say to me, "You've got to be kidding!" She was getting older and at age twelve, was visibly annoyed by more puppy commotion as this new dog and Daisy hit it off immediately. But I had to drive him to the shelter where he might have had a very different fate. The director recognized him as Patches, a dog the shelter had adopted out several weeks before. He had a microchip, so the shelter called his owner, but she said she didn't want him anymore. The shelter kept him for a few days before deciding that he was "too skittish" to be adopted and that this fifteen-month-old dog should be put down the following Monday. So Daisy got a brother, and Patches became Charlie and never had another skittish moment for the rest of his life. By now Lizzie was making it clear the puppies were too much for her, and I was finding Mr. Right more and more annoying. Daisy loved Mr. Right; Charlie loved Daisy, so the three of them made a sweet but noisy family unto themselves.

After a while, Mr. Right wanted to buy a house in another area, a place where I could never have been happy. At this point, Lizzie and I decided we needed a break. Mr. Right and I separated in the most agreeable way and would remain good friends over the years. Mr. Right took Charlie and Daisy with him, and Lizzie and I were finally free to travel. Except for the two trips between Marin and Mount Shasta, Lizzie had never traveled, so I wanted this to be special for her.

I sold all my worldly belongings, packed the trunk of my car, made a bed for Lizzie on the back seat, and on Valentine's Day set off in a snowstorm to visit my daughters in the Bay Area before continuing on to explore the Southwest. We ended up in Utah, and I rented a studio for us. We worked at Best Friends Animal Sanctuary in Kanab for a while, but mostly took day trips all over Utah and Arizona: Zion, Bryce, the Grand Canyon, and Sedona. We met wonderful people, and Lizzie and I had lots of fun. We were like cowgirls. The Southwest was an open range, and all I had to say was "Giddy-up, Lizzie!" and she was in the car, waiting to see where we would go next. After about eight months of traveling, Lizzie was growing tired. It was harder for her to get in and out of the car, so we would stay a few extra days wherever we were so she could rest. Someone had mentioned that New Mexico had a big need for dog people and that there was a large population of wild dogs and also a huge number of people who treated animals cruelly. I was intrigued and felt a calling to go there to see if I could help.

I rented a room with kitchen privileges for Lizzie and myself and planned to stay only three months. I missed my family and friends back in California, and the Southwest had lost its intrigue. I was learning that what I loved most was an alpine home on a lake. The desert was not my cup of tea. But Lizzie never made it to New Mexico. On August 11, she died in her sleep. I was devastated for the fourth time: Taffy, Holly, Tulip—and now Lizzie! It was a helpless feeling to have them one day, and poof, to find them gone—physically, anyway. Lizzie was fifteen and my cowgirl partner. How could I be a cowgirl and continue traveling without her? I realized these dogs held so much of my identity. Their unconditional love, their sweet ways, their different personalities—all that I loved. Each one allowed me to see a little piece of heaven, and each was a great gift to me. This world seemed so tainted without their presence. Every time one of them left, a large part of me wanted to go too.

One of my sweetest memories of Lizzie is what she would do whenever we would stop during our walks so I could talk to someone. Most dogs lie down and wait when people are chatting, but Lizzie would stand behind me, peering out between my legs. This was so cute! As far as I know, the only animals that do that are baby alpacas, who stand between their mothers' front legs and peer out. My Lizzie was the sweetest thing.

Lizzie taught me that I could adapt gracefully in any situation. With her, my cup always felt full. With her, I was a warrior queen, an archetype befitting me. I now know I can do and be anything I want. I have total resilience, and nothing worries me for long. It's actually kind of fun to face a dilemma and to observe myself finding a solution and bouncing back even stronger. As a warrior queen, I have unshakable trust in my ability to lead. I have resilience, poise, and self-assurance.

Lizzie had a beautiful country burial on a beautiful ranch, just like any cowgirl would want. I believed this time my heart would never heal. No more dogs!

Thank you, Lizzie, my sacred teacher!

CHAPTER 6

The Wild Dogs of New Mexico: Bella, Ghost Dog, and Little Doe & Co.

The day after Lizzie's burial, I continued on to New Mexico and stayed for twelve weeks. I ended up in a little town north of Santa Fe, and during my time there, I rescued nine wild dogs and two domestic ones.

From around the world, tourists visit the area where these wild dogs roam. Both are wanderers in this land of adobe houses and of Georgia O'Keefe. As I explored the property that was my temporary home, I saw a few coyotes in the small canyons but no wild dogs. I started to think people had mistaken coyotes for dogs. I came across a fence that separated a canyon from a pasture of cows. Along the fence were the heads of eight coyotes that had been shot. I got sick and ran back to my rented room and called the local shelter. To my horror, someone there assured me this practice was common and legal. I thought I had ended up in hell!

In the days that followed, I would drive by carcasses of deer and elk that had also been beheaded and left on the roadside. This was indeed a violent place. The energy in the state where people like Georgia O'Keefe had lived seemed devoid of anything beautiful. How could this be?

By week three, I still had not seen one wild dog, only coyotes. I heard them howling at night. One night I looked outside to find six sets of lights aimed right at my window; when I looked out again a few minutes later, they were gone. People had said this was a landing place for UFOs, and I know what I saw.

The next day, while walking down the road, I saw two dogs tied to a tree. Two men were yelling at each other. Apparently the dogs had killed the chickens that belonged to one of the men, and by now I could see that both men were very drunk and that the dogs were about to be shot. I screamed at the men that I was a county humane officer and that they should release the dogs and go home. (How I came up with that, I'll never know, and I was also surprised to hear my voice so loud!) When the dogs, both German shepherds, saw me, their tails started wagging. These beautiful dogs were named Sasha and Bella. The first man said only one dog was the "chicken killer." The offender was Bella. I told them I would take Bella off their hands, and she came with me without even a glance back. I called the shelter again and was told the man was within his rights, and anyway, they didn't have room for a large dog. So Bella started sleeping on the floor in my room, but each night, by midnight, she would jump up in bed with me.

The following week I called seven shelters, and the last one put me in touch with a family from Boulder, Colorado, who came to New Mexico to pick her up. Bella started a new life in Colorado—without any chickens. Her new family sent me progress reports, and the last email showed Bella looking very happy. Okay, that was a pretty wild experience, but where were all those wild dogs?

One day, as I walked to my mailbox at the end of a long dirt road, out of nowhere a dog appeared. It would follow me, disappear, show up ahead of me, and then disappear again. I learned from the mail carrier that he was known as Ghost Dog, and was indeed wild and had lived around there on his own, not in a pack, for many years. Families in the neighborhood would toss out feed for their chickens and dog food for Ghost Dog. He never bothered the chickens and so was seen as their protector.

I crossed paths with him many times over the next several weeks, and sometimes he would walk about ten feet away from me and then disappear. One day, I said to him, "So where are all the wild dogs?" Three days later he walked toward me with another dog, a female that looked like a deer. I named her Little Doe. When Ghost Dog disappeared, Little Doe remained and followed me home. I always carried dog food in my car in case it was needed—for instance, by homeless people with dogs—so I set out a little for her in a bowl and also left a bowl of water. Then I went inside for the night. She returned the next day, and this time I put a sleeping bag out with the water and the food. It was snowing when she showed up the next day, so I moved the sleeping bag and the food to the porch. She slept there for about a week but ran off somewhere every morning after she ate.

A few days later I saw her on a ridge and called her by name. When she came to me, I realized she was nursing! I said, "Little Doe, where are your babies?" She ran off, and the next morning she and five tiny puppies were resting comfortably on the sleeping bag. I called the shelter (we were on first-name basis by now), and even though it was closed, someone came out and gently gathered Little Doe and her puppies into a crate. Before I left to return to California, all of the puppies had been adopted and Little Doe had gone home with one of the shelter workers. None of this would have happened if Ghost Dog had not introduced me to her.

The sage is aware of the needs of others.

—Lao Tzu

Little Doe and her puppies would go on to live their lives as pets; they drew just the right people and became beloved members of new families. They would have collars and tags and leashes and pretty bowls with two meals a day and treats. They would have toys and vet visits and baths. Ghost Dog never had any of these things, yet I know he was just as happy, since he had what we all want—total freedom to be who we are.

Ghost Dog was the embodiment of all the wild dogs of New Mexico. He led a simple life, as do I. As a sacred sage, I unclutter my life. I love simplicity. I am grateful for many miracles.

This dog had learned early that if he protected the chickens in the neighborhood, he would be fed. He used all his resources—as I also know how to do—to have a fulfilling life, a life of many freedoms.

Sacred teachers come in all forms; this time my sacred teacher came in matted golden fur with a pink nose. Thank you, Ghost Dog, sacred teacher.

CHAPTER 7

Colin's Story of Compassion

The year before Lizzie and I moved to Utah, I became involved in a large dog- rescue effort. Through the years, I had rescued hundreds of dogs and cats, a horse, a sheep, a burro, and even an iguana, but these were all one-on-one rescues. This was different, and I questioned my sanity through the entire process. While shopping at a feed store, I had overheard people talking about a rescue operation of sorts, owned and mismanaged by a couple well into their eighties. These people said the couple needed a lot of help, since the county was about to shut them down. It was also rumored that they had more than ninety dogs. The operation had 501(c3) nonprofit status and was listed on PetFinders, so at first I thought I might volunteer a few days a month to help out. I called to get directions.

The place was eighty miles away, and I was not prepared for what I saw. There were 149 dogs, including three dead ones lying on the porch of one of the trailers on this ramshackle property! The dogs desperately needed rehousing, since the county was coming within a month to shut down what was essentially a hoarding operation.

They say hoarding animals is a mental illness. I believe it is based on the fear of not having enough love, on the fear that no matter how much one collects, it's never adequate.

There are hoarders who run great big shelters and have the money to provide food for the animals in their care. However, we hear only of the others—the severe cases—on the news. In every case, however, collecting animals points to something lacking. That something is love.

After several weeks of trying to convince the old couple that closing the rescue was for the best, I and six other souls—who had watched the deteriorating situation with great concern—finally got all but a few dogs out of harm's way, since the county would have euthanized most of them. Moving the dogs to other shelters entailed finding a veterinarian willing to vaccinate them so they could travel lawfully, and one of Tulip's legacies came into play: Grace, the veterinarian who visited our house on Tulip's last morning, was the only vet who would come to do it. All the others said they were too busy. After everyone else's vet declined, I called Grace, and this beautiful woman—a goddess—helped me get these dogs to freedom.

My dream was to get every dog out safely. I called dozens of shelters to place them. I had a bit of a rapport with my local shelter and asked if I could bring twelve dogs there. In exchange for the dogs' shelter, I promised that I would be responsible for recruiting assistance for their food and for getting them adopted with the hundred-dollar adoption fee. Homes were found all over the Northwest, and after about six months, there were ten happy endings. Only two dogs remained.

Colin was one of these dogs—a jet-black pit bull with a white tummy, about two years old and scared of everything and everyone. He had been born into the hoarding operation and was put into a corner pen, close to where the old man used to shoot a rifle at night to scare off a mountain lion. Whenever the dogs barked, Colin was one of the first to get sprayed with a water hose, so his young life was frightening. It's no wonder he constantly shook and hung out in the back of his pen at the shelter. People came to see him but found him too shy. I sat with him for many days and took him for little walks in the snow. He was fine with me, relaxed and sweet. He looked like a little bull! I wanted to rename him Ferdinand, but because the shelter had labeled him as a Staffordshire terrier and not as a pit bull, he was stuck with the English-sounding name of Colin.

The shelter would soon tell me that Colin was unadoptable, so I sent his photo to my daughter, who had lost her black Lab three weeks before, and was already searching for another dog. I adopted Colin on Memorial Day weekend to get him out of the shelter and drove him 250 miles to my daughter's house in San Geronimo, California. It was love at first sight! When we arrived, music was playing and I started dancing. Colin circled me a few times, kind of prancing. I never knew he loved music and could dance! (Well, sort of.)

Each time I visit him, we do a little dance. My daughter found a second dog for him so he would have company—Betty Boop, another pit bull—and she and Colin adore one another! Betty Boop has taught Colin how to be a real dog: he swims and loves to go for long walks and to ride in cars. Before, one had to pick him up to get him into the car, and whatever the destination, he would vomit the whole way.

Colin recently turned ten years old, and his favorite thing to do is to snuggle with my daughter as she heals from cancer. He is one of her best medicines, always sweet and precious and a true ambassador for his pit bull breed.

When I worked at Best Friends Rescue in Utah, twenty-two of Michael Vick's fighting dogs arrived after a court ordered that they live out the rest of their lives at this shelter. Vick got two years in prison but was released earlier and was accepted back into the NFL with open arms. Six years later, Alabama's Donnie Anderson, dubbed the godfather of animal abuse, was arrested and 451 of his fighting dogs were seized. Anderson received a sentence of eight years in prison, and most of the dogs had to be euthanized. Are the lives of pit bulls better now? Not yet.

Colin taught me more than anyone about compassion. Here was a pit bull with so many odds against him—born into a hoarding situation, behind only dog fighting, circuses, and zoos in terms of abuse and neglect. He continues to be loving, even though his circumstances could easily have produced a dog that would not have had much will to live, let alone have love to share.

Through Colin, I realized that I had this whole animal cruelty thing wrong. I was judging hoarders and abusers with quiet disdain; in some cases I was nearly in disbelief that people could end up becoming monsters who took advantage of defenseless animals. With these kinds of thoughts, I was actually feeding animal cruelty. People like me, who view this treatment of animals as cruel and reprehensible, are missing the point. What if we stopped referring to "animal cruelty" and thought of ourselves as part of a movement toward love and compassion? Because of Colin, I do not work to stop animal cruelty. Instead, I work in a movement of love and compassion for all animals. The change is simple and facilitates a subtle shift in consciousness. Now, when I speak about the subject, I am heard. The energy of the words "love and compassion for all animals" is so different from the energy of the words "animal cruelty" and of all those terrible images associated with them. And there is no judgment involved, freeing all of us to heal.

Colin embodies the goddess archetype of natural healer. As a natural healer, my insights are precise and relevant. I ask for abundance for my highest good, and I make my points without aggression. When I speak I am heard.

Thank you, Colin, my sacred teacher!

CHAPTER 8

Wyatt's Story of Trust

Wyatt's name at the hoarders' place was Amos, which in Hebrew means "burden." He is an Anatolian shepherd mix and, like Colin, was afraid of everything. He and Colin were the last of the original twelve dogs to be adopted. When I brought him in with the eleven others, he crouched down on his stomach, since he had never been inside a building. He had been transported to the shelter in a horse trailer. Only people who have worked in animal rescue know what it sometimes takes to get a dog from point A to point B. When someone volunteers a vehicle for animal rescue transport— any vehicle—you say yes.

I stayed with Amos for many days, holding all sixty pounds of him on my lap to give him a break from shivering. He had come in with a border collie named Barbie, who was adopted the first week by a family from Portland,

Oregon—322 miles away! He had bunked with Barbie at the hoarders', so not only was he in a strange place, but Barbie had been gone a long time, and I knew he missed her. The shelter finally labeled Amos unadoptable. I talked the staff members out of that three times, but they were losing patience with him and with me. Every time he curled up in my lap, I knew that he wanted to live and that if given the chance, he would be a wonderful pet. He finally did get adopted, but it was the wrong family. On his second day at his new home, these people had left a door open, and now it seemed he was lost for good. But, Pollyanna that I am, I found a silver lining. Wherever Amos had run to—and he had no collar or tags—at least he was out of the shelter, I kept telling myself as I put up fliers with his photo everywhere. I'd had the foresight to take his photo at one point.

Then the light-bulb moment: call an animal communicator! I had relied on them in the past with Lizzie. That's how I found out she thought she would be abandoned when her human mothers cried. So I called Raven Stevens, whom I had met at a park six months earlier, and the magic began. We exchanged many an email, and she was able to get in contact with Amos and to communicate with him. In our emails, we referred to him as "the wanderer."

Subject: Re: The wanderer

From: Adrienne@BandanaCanyon.com, Adrienne@bandana.com

Date: Mon, 09 Apr 2007 at 3:25 PM

To: Raven Stevens flyraven@sbcglobal.net

Nothing new—asked Mike again to keep dogs inside … left my vest there by the front door as he may catch the scent … walked back to the property 2 doors down across the street as Nicky wanted to go there … "feel" he may be under a house? Feel a little too ill to go back tonight but plan to be there early in a.m. unless I feel worse … Given that Amos loves all dogs, I thought this home would be a good one with people that I found out had looked at him a few times, but Emily kept saying he wasn't "ready" to be adopted to them—I didn't know this until last week that they had been wanting him for a long time … Another "reason" they seemed "good" to me … they came back! This has to play out and is much bigger than me—wish I had brought you in to get a better picture of the younger dogs there—actually just his age. I think everyone is doing the best they know how, and I hope the boy knows that he is loved and greatly missed by me … and please tell him that I will find him a better home—just come

back! I am prepared to give Mike
his $100 back (adoption fee and
gift), especially since the boy
can't go back to the shelter …
Hope your back feels better now,
and thank you for coming with me
today! Adrienne

On April 9, 2007, at 4:49 PM, Adrienne@
BandanaCanyon.com wrote:

How early? Whatever you say is
fine, but are we talking 4? 5? 6?
7? I want to be there when he
comes in … Mike said there was
a bear on the roof last October!

Does he want to stay with me? And
my 3 other dogs? That can get
a bit noisy! … Until Jen Mucci
comes back? Forever? What does
he want? Please tell him I am

so sorry for putting him in the wrong house—we had to get him out of the shelter …

If we find him a quiet house with just a person and no dogs, is that better? I will find him whatever he wants— we've come too far to turn around now … but he has to come in so we can provide what he wants …

This is spiritual! As I have no explanation for why I feel so much for this one dog. I love all dogs, but he is loved as though he is one of my own. I know these are all matches made in heaven … I am naming him Sage and starting completely over with his care with your help, and I do want to

pay you for his essences! ... And ...
no more shelter work for me ...
with him that work is completed.
Finally got clarity!

Please tell him he doesn't have
to live with those people. It's
taken months to feel this clear
about my not going back to the
shelter. He is one of my best
teachers! I will call him softly
(Amos for now) as my voice is
going in and out.

Thanks! Again ... Oh how I hope he
shows up, though I know there
is often a bigger picture that
we can't always see ... will do my
best. Adrienne

Raven Stevens wrote:

Take good care of yourself. If you can be there in the early morning and just wait quietly … no dogs (I think not even Nikki), no family … just you. And use your voice softly. He trusts you!

Have them call us as soon as they spot him again. And have one person go after him if we are not around. With no dogs.

I am getting a "view" of where he is. He is away from dogs … he says. I have asked him to go back to the house. He says they don't "get it"! Telling him we will find the right place for him and to come in …

Trusting … Raven

Paws for Reflection

An Animal Communication and Healing Practice

www.paws4reflection.net

Subject: Re: The wanderer

From: Adrienne@BandanaCanyon.com, Adrienne@bandana.com

Date: Tue, 10 Apr 2007 06:07:54-0700

To: Raven Stevens flyraven@sbcglobal.net

Yes I will. Let's talk. A "knowing" friend in Sacramento said he will come back but only to bolt again … this is clearly not his home—will explain all as soon as I have him in my car and safe!

Raven Stevens wrote:

> Whatever time you can get there …
> he will be around. He is lurking
> close by. Just keep everyone else
> away … call me when you have him.
>
> Bayla said we can have him here
> in the yard and garage if it works
> for Dakota and Mylo. Sleeping in
> the house might not work with the
> cat … I can't commit to doing it
> long term but short term … Jen
> will be back May 15 … would you
> still work with him and take him
> to adoption days, etc.? Let's talk
> about it some more, ok?
>
> But I agree, he really can't go
> back to the shelter … and I like
> the name Sage. All is well … keep
> breathing and trust. Raven

Paws for Reflection

An Animal Communication and Healing Practice

www.paws4reflection.net

Subject: All hugs and kisses

From: Adrienne@BandanaCanyon.com, Adrienne@bandana.com

Date: Tue, 10 Apr 2007 08:46:44-0700

To: Raven Stevens flyraven@sbcglobal.net

Got there at 7:08 and by 7:30 he was in my car … all hugs and kisses—he looks gorgeous. Fed him and parked out in front of your house for an hour—too early to wake you. He will rest/sleep in my car for an hour or so—then I have to call Mike and Debra and

```
report to the Humane that he is

found … Then?
```

So Raven communicated with Amos, and on his fourth day out, he agreed to meet me the next morning in the woods where he was hiding. She said to call his name softly and he would come to me. I arrived just after dawn, and as I called softly, many animals emerged from the woods and ran past me: deer, an old raccoon, a fox, and a bobcat. I heard a great deal of rustling behind me, and I was sure my calling had awakened a bear, which were common in that neighborhood. But then I saw Amos! I got down on my knees with my arms outstretched, and he ran right to me. We fell together in a huge hug on the forest floor. He quickly got into my car and devoured the bowl of food I had brought for him. After a few laps of water, he was fast asleep on the back seat as we drove away. I called Raven, the animal communicator, and she said he could come to her place, and if Dakota, her old dog; Mylo, her cat, and Bayla, her partner, agreed, then Amos could stay in their garage while she and I worked at getting him the right home.

A month passed and we still had not come up with the right fit. Then Amos found the best home any dog could ever want: Raven's! And one of the best parts is that I can visit him anytime. His new home is beautiful and filled with love. He has two mamas, Raven and Bayla, and when he turned six, he gained a brother. Raven had seen Chester on *The Bonnie Hunt Show*, knew he was hers, and drove from Mount Shasta to Los Angeles to pick him up. So Amos had Chester and a cat named Mylo to grow up with.

I have been their pet sitter many times—once for three weeks when their mamas went to Italy. I'm known in the house as Auntie A. We changed Amos's name to Wyatt, which suited him far better than the name Sage.

Whenever Wyatt's mamas and I share emails, we always add "sp-sp-sp," which means "smoochie the poochie." It's like blowing kisses to our dogs!

That fateful morning so long ago, Wyatt taught me about trust. He trusted that I would be there for him, and I trusted him to hear me. He now hikes off leash and is the poster boy for all my rescue work. His framed photo has a special place on my writing desk. Our bond is immense. I can see a golden light of energy between us when we cuddle. Wyatt brought out my daring-diva goddess archetype. As a daring diva, I am authentic and connected to my intuition and am always aware of my inner tigress and prepared for success.

Because Wyatt trusted me, I understand that to put my trust in God is the same as trusting myself, and I trust myself completely. Whatever decision I make is the right one for me. When you trust yourself, you feel whole. I never doubt myself, my purpose, or any part of my life, and I never worry about where I'll end up next. I always have me, and I can count on me. This is freedom. I am in a league of my own. I don't need to compare or to compete with anyone. I speak my mind, and I walk my talk. Wyatt and I did together what no one thought possible. Now, whenever I have little doubts or little troubles, I speak softly to God and I have total trust that I am heard. Thank you, Wyatt, sacred teacher, for this gift.

CHAPTER 9

Dakota Blue's Story of Healing

There is no path to happiness;

happiness is the path.

—Buddha

On a sunny Saturday in 2008, people from all over the world gathered in Barcelona, Spain, to listen to Deepak Chopra speak at the Alliance for a New Humanity conference. During his talk, he said that earlier that morning, he had taken a vow of nonviolence. Back in the 1980s, I had taken a similar vow, but only in my heart. I had never spoken it aloud, but it involved my wish to do whatever I could to help bring peace to the planet. I stopped eating all meat, and I started helping animals find safe havens whenever I could. I felt the call many times, not just to adopt animals but to help others adopt and to get involved in the hands-on activity of animal rescue.

A few years later, I adopted a cow and a bull, naming them Satori and Anand. Satori recently became a mother, so that makes me a grandma! Initially their home was in Georgia at the Sacred Cows Sanctuary, and I helped with their expenses each month. However, due to recent threats from the owner of the land that the sanctuary rents, Anand was moved to a sanctuary in Florida. Anand and Satori will live out their lives in peace and never have to endure the trauma of being transported to a slaughterhouse. Sponsoring them makes me feel peaceful, and it aligns me with my purpose, which is to spread the messages of love, peace, compassion, and nonviolence wherever I go.

Their photos are framed and sit on my writing desk to remind me to pray that others will take their own vows of nonviolence as they awaken to their purposes. Peace is healing. When we are peaceful as a nation, as a neighborhood, or as individuals, we are healed. Taking a vow of nonviolence is a way to heal the planet.

With yet another partner, I moved back to California from the Southwest to a sweet town in the Sierra foothills.

The first day there, after finding a rental home and signing a lease, I decided to visit the local animal shelter to see if I could volunteer. Barney was a little gray terrier mix who was deaf and needed special care. I had worked with deaf dogs before, so my plan was to walk him each day. This would also allow me to get some exercise and to meet new friends with common interests. Three weeks into it, Barney got adopted. Another dog, Spring, clearly needed exercise, and for six weeks I walked her, making friends along the way. In addition, I was teaching my tele-classes to empower women and spending summer days in the lake basin, surrounded by nature.

My trips to the shelter to walk dogs and to take puppies to puppy classes now became my daily morning ritual—a way to give back and to be around dog energy. However, I made it abundantly clear that although I loved to volunteer, I was no longer in a position to adopt another dog.

Several weeks passed, and one day I entered the kennel area and came upon a dog I had never seen before: a huge Akita/German shepherd mix that had been returned, since he needed hip surgery and the family that adopted him a year before could not afford the cost. These people wanted a dog that could accompany them on long runs and hikes, and Dakota was diagnosed with hip dysplasia. Initially, there were three surgical options for him, but when more tests were done, the vet found that only a partial fix could be performed due to the abnormal bone structure that had developed in Dakota's first year of life. This meant that Dakota would always be labeled as a special-needs dog and would be severely limited in how far he could walk or run.

He had the surgery and needed three months of rest and rehab in a quiet foster home while he healed. So, two weeks after his surgery, he was back at the shelter, and the staff members were looking high and low for a foster home. They asked me, but I said no. They asked me again, and again I said no. I had rescued many a dog needing a temporary home, and I knew how hard it was to find a good foster home. I had found perhaps forty such homes at the height of my rescue career, so when they asked me a third time, I said yes!

My earlier dogs were gone, my daughters were settled and married, and my parents had passed. I had no responsibilities except to myself, so why not? Wasn't this the least I could do for twelve weeks of my life? I was done traveling—for the time being, anyway. I had met a wonderful man and had settled in. I had a thriving part-time business, so I had plenty of time. Besides, I have always loved a good challenge. I had seen this situation play out dozens of times with other dogs. At the end of twelve weeks, the shelter staff asked me to bring Dakota back so he could be put up for adoption. I could not and would not even dream of living without Dakota, even though my partner said he didn't think it was the right time for us to have a dog. I felt differently, of course. Dakota was mine and I was his, and we were joined at his broken hip!

I gave him the last name Blue, and Dakota Blue will be five years old this year. I'm not sure of his birth date, but it is sometime in May. I like May 19, since nineteen is a ten and a one in numerology and symbolizes perfection and completion. To me Dakota is the perfect dog. His size alone says majesty, his golden coat is soft, and he stays clean even without baths, although he swims all summer long. He has beautiful white teeth and in a word is handsome. He doesn't know that or that he is big or has white teeth; he doesn't care. He just knows that I love him and that he is Dakota Blue, and that's all that seems important to him with one exception: he knows about wrapped presents! At Christmastime he somehow knows which gifts are his and can sniff them out, and like Holly, Tulip, and Lizzie, he unwraps them himself with much delight and enthusiasm. It's the same on his birthday. He just knows. Maybe Dakota does this to make me happy, since I love watching this little drama unfurl every year.

When I'm interviewing new clients to see if they are a match for my classes, I often ask them if they celebrate their pets' birthdays, and each woman has said no. As all my dogs, particularly Dakota Blue, have shown me, a little whimsy in life makes it so much richer. People miss out when the silly stuff goes right by them. Any opportunity to give makes life far more special. Dakota gets a new toy even on his adoption date, September 15! It's another way for me to honor this fabulous being who has blessed my life.

I love Dakota Blue—all 120 pounds of him—and he loves to walk, swim, hike, and play in the snow. He still eats his meals out of my hand, a habit that started when he was recovering from his hip surgery. And with every bite of food he takes, I pray for his continued health and happiness. Like no one else, he has shown me how to step into the flow of life. Of all the goddess archetypes, his alone has shown me my magic! I have become the best version of myself because of him.

As a magical muse, I rule over my creativity. I can step into the flow while maintaining my sense of purpose. I relish beauty and grace.

Dakota Blue is my message of healing. After his surgery, I was told he would be on painkillers like Rimadyl for the rest of his life. He has never needed one. Our bodies can heal on their own over time with proper nutrition and a lifestyle that meets our passions and brings us joy. This is how I've raised Dakota Blue. He has never needed another veterinarian appointment. He was over-vaccinated in the shelter and during his surgery, and I could see those toxins in his energy fields. Remember, I'm all about energy! In his first weeks of healing, I played a lot of music in a frequency that seemed to match his. It was a DNA healing tone at 432 Hz. I believe that there are secret miracle healing codes in music and that many truths can be found in sound. Often, when I'm listening to 528 Hz meditation music, Dakota Blue "sings" along with it— a softer version of his moonlight howl, "Arroooh." I would love to see veterinarians and animal shelters play soothing 432 Hz music for the animals in their care.

As he approaches his fifth year, Dakota Blue is vibrant and quite the lover of all: cats, deer, rabbits, birds, horses, cows, little children, all women, and most men. In all the joy that Dakota Blue is, I have expanded my own level of joy, and the feeling is contagious! My life is all about compassion, and somehow I have manifested this beautiful being into my life. The world is a beautiful place.

After leaving New Mexico, I could have moved anywhere, but I was drawn to the Sierras, to that small rescue organization, and ultimately to my Dakota Blue. I thank him often, telling him he didn't have to come with a broken hip to get my attention. Then we hug and roll around; I laugh and he snorts like a great horse, and the energy in my house is golden with happiness! Dakota Blue has brought Colin's message to me many times: true compassion leads to exquisite happiness. With Dakota Blue, I have more peace than at any other time in this life. A mind at peace, a mind centered and not focused on harming others, is stronger than any physical force in the universe.

I no longer give my attention to violence against animals. I focus my attention on my own path: compassion for all. I've learned that dedicating my time to being against animal cruelty is the same as dedicating my life to something I hate. I was, in the past, feeding it with my energy by focusing on cruelty issues.

As my journey has continued and my dogs, from Taffy to Dakota Blue, have gifted me with their teachings, I have learned to use what I am against to decide what I am for and to put all of my focus, time, passion, and energy into that. Now I say, "I am for compassion for all souls." This is a softer way to save animals, and I can still champion my cause but now from the standpoint of love. I try to bring my goddess energy to all whom I meet. I am certain that Dakota Blue has more to teach me, and like all my sacred teachers in fur, I thank him for finding me, for rescuing me, and for showing me every day that my life's purpose is all about experiencing joy.

I am finally at peace with myself and love myself completely, and Dakota Blue reflects that. Animals are always themselves. They never lose touch with their essence and never resist love. They want to live or they would not be here. We've all seen the tiniest kitten hold on to life.

The moon is my ruler in astrology, and during the full moon I engage in prayer more often than during the other phases. As I wait for the moon each month, Dakota Blue assigns himself a seat on the floor in front of the window. As I begin my prayers, he starts to howl. It's a sound that catches my breath, a far memory sound, perhaps of wolves communicating—and I love it! It starts low and builds into a beautiful, almost conch-like sound. Dakota's eyes are closed and his mouth forms a perfect circle. His lungs must be mammoth! The cry lasts for about a minute, and then he settles at my feet. I don't know if he is picking up my energy or the moon's energy or if this is his call to prayer, but it's one of the most beautiful sounds on the planet: Aroooh! Aroooh!

Aroooh is Dakota Blue's word for "No soul is more sacred than another."

Dakota Blue is a lover first, and by that I mean he loves everyone. I have watched him communicate with deer. If we are out on a walk and one appears perhaps fifty feet away, he sits and quietly stares. The deer stops eating and stares back. This can go on for up to twenty minutes. The deer always moves on first. After such an encounter, I always feel I have landed in some of Dakota Blue's bliss. Time just stops. I know my inner child is happy and healthy, and Dakota Blue's inner puppy seems to be the same way. We both know we are totally validated. Videos of unlikely animal pairs have become popular on the Internet. A pig nestles against a house cat. A goat frolics with a baby rhinoceros. A bear, a lion, and a tiger that have been together since they were young are still the best of friends. Scientists are beginning to say that different species are capable of communication with each other. I will go so far as to say that all animals have spirit guides, just like we do. Many unseen forces are helping all of us to expand our consciousness, and animals are also expanding theirs.

To see things in the seed, that is genius.

—Lao Tzu

My prayer is that we all focus on what we want and not on what we fear and that we give all our animals daily kisses and hugs and thanks for finding us!

I have learned on my journey that animals can teach us all to love, but before we can love others, we must first learn to love ourselves. To love ourselves is to become the source of our own happiness. Animals seem to be in complete harmony with themselves, and we are all connected to one another in universal energy of love. It's so simple. Love is all there is!

The world would change completely if everyone could conceive of a life without violence. Wars would end, all animals would be universally loved and respected, and children would regain their birthright of freedom. I love to imagine what this would feel like. Sometimes, while sitting in my beautiful alpine yard on a sunny afternoon, listening to the silences between bird's songs, I close my eyes and pray for this world to be at peace without duality.

As my eyes open, I look at my seventh sacred teacher, my magical muse, my huge, beautiful, handsome bundle of love, and Dakota Blue shifts ever so slightly as he looks back at me. Our eyes meet, as they often do these days, and we hold our gaze as if to say, "I know someday there will be peace for all!"

EPILOGUE

All my years of searching have brought me back full circle: I am who I was searching for!

Thirty-five years of life with my dogs; thirty-five years of traveling the world; thirty-five years of a plant-based diet, looking for wholeness, health, and true abundance in simplicity—these are all the paths I took along my journey, and I found the greatest treasure was me, my authentic self.

All religions lead back to the source. All the ascended masters have something to teach us, and the message throughout the ages has always been the same: know your true self and know that the source of all energy is everywhere and especially within each one of us. Love is all there has ever been, is now, and ever will be. The rest is illusion. As Meher Baba said, "Don't worry. Be happy!" Life is simple once you know your purpose. My grandmother always told me, "Do your best and be kind to all, and life will unfold in wondrous ways."

The part of me that I couldn't reach in my younger years was the part recognizing that God (source energy) was within me. Other than the beauty of the robes and the ceremonies, the church seemed empty to me. I never needed to go guru shopping all over Asia or to join any sect. I did not find a teacher or a guru, and I sometimes wonder if would I appreciate my life more completely and know what I know now if I had aligned with some particular path. Either way, I love my life and how it continues to unfold. I am grateful because I am blessed to live a simple life, steeped in compassion and love.

> **I belong to no religion. My religion**
> **is love. Every heart is my temple.**
> **—Jalāl ad-Dīn Muhammad Rūmī**

I don't need to defend anything. I am not what I have. I am not what I do. I am not what other people think of me. I give away everything I can in gratitude, and I continue to live my life as simply and freely as possible. I am compassion and love. I live in peace and total joy.

"Om mani peme hung" is a beautiful Tibetan mantra available to anyone who feels inspired to develop great love and compassion. Many associate this mantra with the Dalai Lama, as he is said to be the reincarnation of the Buddha of compassion.

I am goddess living.

I am goddess loving.

I am goddess divine.

And so it is—from orphan to goddess, all the way home.

The End

PART III

ACKNOWLEDGMENTS

Thanks to all my dear ones who supported me with their love as I put this book together.

My best friends and my daughters are not only physically beautiful women but have always believed in something higher than themselves, which encompasses who they are. Their love for animals is intense, and their energy is contagious and divine! They are smart and aware, awakening to their own sacred truths more and more each day, and applying these truths to their lives.

I thank Debbie, Bayla, Cynthia, Loree, Raven, Gina, Susan, Malaya, Julie in Wisconsin, Julie in Hawaii, and my daughters, Celina and Layla, for encouraging me to write my story and for being in the world at this time with me. They are goddesses in every way! I love them all with oceans of love.

I am especially grateful to Cynthia Henderson for typing the manuscript that has become this book and especially for her wisdom and gentle editorial comments, which created a more magical flow many times. I also thank the staff at BalboaPress, a division of Hay House, for helping me launch my book in the world of self-publishing, which has been a wonderful experience.

And, yes, of course there is a divine masculine.

I love men! I thank all my male friends, my lovers, my boyfriends, and my ex-husband. They have all helped me to be the goddess that I am. They are all divine masculine in their own special ways and will remain treasures in my heart forever. I thank them for complementing my divine feminine.

Because of my experiences as a woman, this book stresses the attributes of the divine feminine, but I am clearly aware that the divine feminine and the divine masculine reside within every one of us.

For the purposes of this book, I have focused on the divine feminine and the goddess archetypes as they have presented themselves within each of the dogs and on my experiences with them.

RESOURCES

The following organizations and individuals have my undying love and respect for the work they do to help animals know they are safe and loved.

Alpine Veterinary Hospital
Grace Roberts, DVM
Weed, California 96094

Cape Center for Animal
Protection
and Education,
J. P. Novik, owner
Santa Cruz, California
Grass Valley, California

High Sierra Animal Rescue
Doug and Betty Rodriguez,
owners
Portola, California
www.HighSierra
AnimalRescue.org

Paws for Reflection
Raven Stevens, animal
communicator
Mount Shasta, California
www.Paws4Reflection.net

Peace Pigs Sanctuary
Judy Woods, owner
Stanwood, Washington

Sacred Cows Sanctuary
Susan Rajan and Malaya
Stephans
Gainesville, Georgia

The Heart and Soul
Sanctuary
Natalie Owings, owner
Glorietta, New Mexico
505-757-6817

Gunyah Animal Healing
Sanctuary
Kathy Munslow, founder
Victoria, Australia
www.gunyah.org

The following people are shamans who live in Southern California and work remotely with people all over the world. They send out intense love and wellness and are connected with source energy. A session with any of them is like being cocooned in a warm blanket. It feels good and the results are beautiful, often lingering for days and weeks. These are gentle, kind beings, doing what they came here to do. They are healers and never take you anywhere you don't feel you're prepared to go.

Carrie Hart

Carrie's truth is crystal clear and is conveyed through her music as well as her words. She also works closely with the animal kingdom. Carrie leads power gatherings via MaestroConference.

For information about Carrie, see the following sites:

www.I-Am-This.com

www.PowerAnimalsUnleashed.com

www.Quado.com

David Rafael Issacson

David offers intensive healings. All one has to do is sit quietly in

one's own home, and the work is done remotely. In a word, David

is amazing. I always feel young and endless after a healing session with him.

For information about David, go to:

www.SpiritPortal.org

Katie Weatherup

Katie does it all: retreats to faraway places like England and Scotland, illumination healings, soul retrievals, and Reiki. She exudes a fresh sweetness, with plenty of remote hugs that one can actually feel.

For more information, go to:

Katie@HandsOverHeart.com

Thank you. I love you all!

MY BUCKET LIST

I came to Earth this time to:

- ✓ Get adopted
- ✓ Be a daughter
- ✓ Grow up in New England, USA
- ✓ Be a granddaughter
- ✓ Move to Berkeley, California, at age eighteen
- ✓ Go to college
- ✓ Marry once
- ✓ Become a wife
- ✓ Become a mother twice
- ✓ Study theology, Sufism, metaphysics, Huna
- ✓ Travel to India
- ✓ Travel to China, Japan, Burma, and Thailand
- ✓ Travel to Canada
- ✓ Travel to Mexico
- ✓ Fly around the world twice
- ✓ Live and work in Hawaii
- ✓ Travel to thirty-eight states in the USA, including Alaska
- ✓ Build a dog park
- ✓ Become a vegetarian and a vegan

- ✓ Always have my own dog companion
- ✓ Design a country home
- ✓ Fall in love at least five times
- ✓ Work in an art gallery in Sausalito, California
- ✓ Always be able to buy books
- ✓ Become a published writer
- ✓ Work as a cook in a vegetarian restaurant
- ✓ Own a K-9 walking/ hiking/pet-sitting service
- ✓ Own and operate a K-9 cookie business
- ✓ Work in dog rescue
- ✓ Own a space clearing company
- ✓ Teach empowerment tele-classes to women
- ✓ Work in the state of Utah at Best Friends Animal Sanctuary
- ✓ Meet ten women who have become lifelong friends
- ✓ Become a minister in the Universal Life Church Monastery
- ✓ Adopt and sponsor a sanctuary cow and bull and name them Satori and Anand
- ✓ Work with shamans for healings

✓ Write a book about my journey from orphan to goddess

✓ Find the meaning of life

And the list continues:

- Become initiated in Munay-Ki
- Join Humanity's Team (an international spiritual movement, the purpose of which is to communicate and demonstrate the timeless Truth, that we are One.)
- Continue learning everything I can about sacred geometry
- See the phrase *animal cruelty* replaced by the term *animal compassion*
- Open shelters across the United States for homeless people with dogs
- Keep expanding my awareness

A DREAM

In January 2015 Blueberry Barn appeared in a dream. It is the writing studio I have always wanted—a beautiful barn painted in shades of blue: indigo, turquoise, royal blue, and aqua. This dream affirmed that my writing studio was on its way.

A few days later, I made that nighttime dream into a day dream. As I sat in my alpine garden with Dakota Blue, I imagined inviting thirty-three people to Blueberry Barn for a vegan feast catered by the Living Café on the Mendocino coast of California. Yes, I realize that café is four hundred miles from where I live, but this is my day dream, so time and distance have no meaning. This is an example of how I bring joy to myself. I love thinking about Blueberry Barn and planning my ultimate party of joy and gratitude.

My guest list includes the mystics and mentors who continue to inspire me. I thank them all for their wisdom.

They are the light keepers of the universe, and the earth is so fortunate to have them here! I have invited those who have dropped their bodies as of this writing (*), since their wisdom and presence are still felt ever so strongly.

MY GUEST LIST

Louise Hay

Mike Dooley

Alan Watts*

Jo Jayson

Ralph Smart

Derek Walcott

Teal Swan

Deepak Chopra

Marianne
Williamson

Gary Zukov

Sylvia Browne*

Neale Donald
Walsh

Thomas Moore

Byron Katie

Will Tuttle

Lisa Thiel

Dr. Wayne Dyer

Paulo Coello

Doreen Virtue

Carlos Santana

Dan Millman

Maya Angelou*

Martha Beck

Iyanla Vanzant

Stuart Wilde*

Don Miguel Ruis

Mary Oliver

Ester Hicks

Valerie Love

Eckhart Tolle

Geri Larkin

Ruth
Armington*

His Holiness, the
Dalai Lama

Can you imagine how Blueberry Barn would shimmer with love? My date for the evening would be Davidji and he could bring his beloved dog Peaches to keep Dakota Blue company.

A POEM

My Quiet Faith

Now I am honest.

Now I am kinder.

Listened to the goddess.

Now I stand behind her.

Being true to me

has set my love free.

Everywhere I am looking, love grows,

and that's all you need to know.

The rest is ancient his-tory.

Am living in the now, not looking back at me.

The intricacies of my story would take twenty-five books.

There's so much more to life than how it looks.

For years and years have gone very deep.

Now loving my stillness. No need to leap.

I have my quiet faith

and my ultimate trust

in God and my dogs, and that's enough.

—written at Lake Tahoe, 2012

A PRAYER

Dear Mother and Father God,

Please bless the animals in farm sanctuaries and shelters everywhere. May your blessed light shine upon their sweet and innocent faces. They have made it through the storms, and the cold hearts are far behind them. May the dark rain of their tears turn to sunshine. Please bless them so they may know that their lives matter and that they all spring from the same mother and can live in unity, peace, joy, and the truth of their sacredness. They are healing the world by teaching compassion. May we all open our hearts and walk with the animals, guided by the sacred light in their eyes.

Dear Mother and Father God, thank you for blessing the animals in farm sanctuaries and shelters everywhere.

They are ambassadors of peace.

They are loved.

They are love!

Amen.

ABOUT THE AUTHOR

Adrienne Gallant lives and works surrounded by nature in the American Northwest. Her days are spent writing, listening to music, painting, meditating, reading, daydreaming, walking, and praying. She has named her home the Place Beyond Seeking and has furnished it in what she describes as Zen chic.

She teaches and inspires many women to empower themselves via weekly tele-classes and also offers special blessings to residents of animal shelters, rescue homes, and farm sanctuaries.

Adrienne is studying sacred geometry and is continuing her writing career. You can contact Adrienne at www. adriennegallant.com.

Printed in the United States
By Bookmasters